SAGGISTICA 31

INTERROGATIONS INTO ITALIAN-AMERICAN STUDIES
The Francesco and Mary Giambelli Foundation Lectures

Mary and Francesco Giambelli at their restaurant, Giambelli 50th

INTERROGATIONS INTO ITALIAN-AMERICAN STUDIES

The Francesco and Mary Giambelli
Foundation Lectures

Edited by
Anthony Julian Tamburri

BORDIGHERA PRESS

Library of Congress Control Number: 2019937315

© 2020 by the Authors

All rights reserved. Parts of this book may be reprinted only by written permission from the author, and may not be reproduced for publication in book, magazine, or electronic media of any kind, except for purposes of literary reviews by critics.

Printed in the United States.

Published by
BORDIGHERA PRESS
John D. Calandra Italian American Institute
25 West 43rd Street, 17th Floor
New York, NY 10036

SAGGISTICA 31
ISBN 978-1-59954-143-3

TABLE OF CONTENTS

ix	Acknowledgements
xi	Giambelli Foundation • "Preface"
xiii	Anthony Julian Tamburri • "Introduction"
1	Fred l. Gardaphé • "In Education Begin Responsibilities. Or, Why Italian Americans Don't Know What They Don't Know"
35	Maria Laurino • "Lessons from Once Dangerous Americans"
53	Donna R. Gabaccia • "Virtual Sambuca: Research in Rural Sicily Before and After the Digital Revolution"
103	Robert Viscusi • "The Orphanage: Encounters in Transnational Space"
129	Index

Acknowledgments

This volume is the result of a most generous grant by the Francesco and Mary Giambelli Foundation. Under the presidency of Angelo Vivolo, the Giambelli Foundation provided the necessary resources for the John D. Calandra Italian American Institute to organize four lectures during the calendar year 2017, which were then collected for this volume.

In addition to the Foundation's president, we are also pleased and honored to thank Justine Tenny and Claudio DeVellis, Board members who made the decision together with Angelo Vivolo to fund this and yet another project of the John D. Calandra Italian American Institute.

In these past few years, the Francesco and Mary Giambelli Foundation has proven to be among the very few Italian/American foundations most cognizant of the need to support those projects that delve deeper into the history and culture of Italians in America. The Giambelli Foundation has exhibited a most significant and perceptive thought process on the importance of historical and cultural support.

While the number of Italian/American associations, foundations, and NGOs is significant, very few match the scope of donations to social and cultural projects that the Giambelli Foundation has exhibited to date.

Anthony Julian Tamburri
August 2019

PREFACE

Francesco Giambelli was born in 1915 in Voghera, outside Milan, Italy. Across the ocean in America, in Brooklyn, New York, Mary Anzalone was born one year later. Francesco started working at restaurants at the age of ten and worked in various hotels in his hometown as a waiter until he was 17. He then went to Milan to the famed Savini's Ristorante, and then onto various restaurants in Rome and Siena. Mary meanwhile pursued her education in the New York City school system. She became a secretary and eventually an associate designer in the women's millinery field in New York.

In 1937, Francesco went to Leipzig, Germany and while working in the restaurant industry there, he soon learned to speak German. Through other jobs in Monte Carlo, France and England, he learned to speak French and English as well. In 1949, with all the experience he acquired in various restaurants in different countries, Francesco returned to his hometown of Voghera and opened his own restaurant, "Il Pesce d'Or," which soon became a success. In 1954 he sold that restaurant and immigrated to America.

Francesco and Mary met one year later, marking the beginning of a remarkable personal and professional partnership. In 1956, Francesco opened Giambelli's Ristorante on Madison Avenue and 37th Street in New York, and then in 1960, sold that location and opened Giambelli's 50th Ristorante on 50th Street near St. Patrick's Cathedral.

Over the years, Giambelli's 50th served many distinguished personalities, including presidents of the United States and other countries. Its clientele included kings, queens, and other royalty, theatrical and motion picture celebrities, politicians and business executives. While all enjoyed the exquisite cuisine and fine wines served by the Giambellis, the secret to their success was the incredibly warm and welcoming atmosphere they extended to each and every guest, which came from a sincere and genuine concern for others.

One of the highlights for the Giambellis was Pope John Paul II's historic trip to New York City in October 1995. They generously hosted and had the privilege of serving the Holy Father and his guests of 50 Cardinals at the residence of Cardinal O'Connor at St. Patrick's Cathedral.

Taking to heart the words "not the least of my brethren," Francesco and Mary demonstrated a lifetime of generosity toward those in need. On regular basis, Francesco and Mary contributed food and funds to the Cardinal's program for feeding the homeless and made substantial contributions to many charitable organizations. They established the Francesco and Mary Giambelli Foundation with the intention of creating a legacy that would continue their lifetime charitable intentions and promote the ideals of Italian American Culture.

This lecture series and book publication are just two of the many projects the Giambelli Foundation continues to fund. Among other cultural programs we can include the support of the only Italian/American television program, *Italics*, or the significant donation to the memorial of the Triangle Shirtwaist factory monument in New York City. All of this and more constitute an inimitable legacy in Italian American Culture.

Board of Trustees
Francesco and Mary Giambelli Foundation
August 2019

INTRODUCTION
Cultural Philanthropy, A Private Affair

Anthony Julian Tamburri

In his ground-breaking essay, "Breaking the Silence: Strategic Imperatives for Italian American Culture," Robert Viscusi championed an articulation of history that includes a collective purpose.[1] While much progress has been made on numerous issues, many Italian American associations seem to work in a vacuum, moving forward alone on issues whereas, within groups working in unison, the community at large would benefit, thus encountering greater success in bringing forth a variety of projects that would contribute to an Italian/American agenda.

What is—or, what should be—that rallying point around which the greater Italian/American population might find some sense of commonality? Indeed, both African Americans and Jewish Americans have their one issue, as tragic as it may be, that coheres the group. I have in mind, of course, slavery and its dreadful sister of outright discrimination that has resulted from it, for the former; two millennia of *diasporic* existence and the more recent horrific holocaust, for the latter. What then can we identify as that cohesive force for Italian Americans? Can we look to something as immigration, that timespan 1880 to 1924, those forty-four years that have now become an historical marker for contemporary Italian Americans? There may indeed be specific tragedies that come to mind: the 1891 New Orleans lynching, for which we hold the dubious distinction of having been victims of the largest group lynching.[2] One might even underscore historical discrimination,

---

[1] See his essay in *Voices in Italian Americana* 1.1 (Spring 1990): 1-13.
[2] After one hundred twenty-eight years, the City of New Orleans issued a formal apology for such a heinous act. For details on this event, see Ryan Prior's article, "128 years later, New Orleans is apologizing for lynching 11 Italians" CNN.

dating back to the nineteenth century and culminating, to date, in something like *Everyone Loves Raymond* or *The Sopranos*.

Though valid points of discussion, these last two examples do not constitute, in an encompassing manner, that one issue that can unite the Italian/American population in the same way in which other groups cohere. We might thus ponder what is that all encompassing issue that unites, for instance, Hispanic Americans. In addition to a strong sense of belonging they may have with regard to their culture(s), it may very well be the migratory experience—a sense of not belonging to the host country—that coheres Hispanics.

Surely, I do not want to be naïve in thinking that Hispanics from any and all Latin countries have an equal sense of allegiance to the "old country." Nor do I want to imply that all Hispanics have an automatic sense of belonging to that group comprised of Hispanics/Latinos, as categorized in the United States. Nevertheless, we would not err in perceiving a certain sense of commonality that has its origins in the migratory experience insofar as they perceive themselves as outsiders, and, as such, hold on to their culture of origins. This combination of difference and cultural specificity—based in part on the migratory experience—surely figures as a cohering agent.

A similar formula might prove valid for Italian Americans. Immigration and its century-long history may very well figure as that cohesive agent, however tenuous. A strong sense of commonality is that necessary ingredient for the population to cohere and this to progress, for the study of all things Italian/American to

---

https://www.cnn.com/2019/04/01/us/new-orleans-mayor-apologizes-italian-americans-trnd/index.html. Indeed, we had to wait for an African American female mayor in order to have someone in office who could truly empathize with this historical tragedy. For more on the lynchings of Italian in the United States, see Patrizia Salvetti's *Rope and Soap: Lynchings of Italians in the United States*. Trans. Fabio Girelli Carasi (New York: Bordighera Press, 2017).

become part and parcel of the dominant culture, as it is for other United States hyphenated groups.

All of this is dependent on an Italian/American commitment (*impegno*) to the appreciation of our culture. This entails an active participation in cultural activities of all sorts; it requires that Italian/American groups make a concerted effort to go beyond those one or two activities they have identified as their own, and make attempts to expand their agenda to include a new, more encompassing form of cultural integration. All of this, as we shall see, is dependent on a combination of cultural awareness and appreciation: namely a new sense of the Italian/American self that ultimately leads to an appropriation of one's cultural legacy.

A concerted *conversation* (i.e., coming together) on cultural philanthropy among/by Italian Americans is, I would submit, something necessary to bring to the table. The concept has yet to be discussed beyond those few occasions among a small number of individuals. We need only turn to (1) names on libraries, colleges of arts and humanities, and privately endowed professorships, (2) the lack of a free-standing national museum, and (3) graduate programs in Italian Americana for us to realize how far behind we are in cultural appreciation.

Education is the main way we can change people's minds. Italian Americans must step up to the plate and support grand projects such as a worthy Italian/American museum at the national level, endowed professorships and centers, as well as other entities and/or institutions dedicated to imparting knowledge of our history and culture. This ultimately brings us to the dire need of private, cultural philanthropy; there is a lack of Italian/American names on (1) college and university libraries, (2) colleges of arts and humanities, and (3) endowed professorships, just to name a few areas.

Less than a dozen names come to mind when discussing private, cultural philanthropy vis-à-vis Italian and Italian/American Studies: UNICO National has established to date six chairs in

Italian/American Studies, beginning in 1987 with the Emiliana Pasca Noether Chair in Modern Italian History at the University of Connecticut.[3] Baroness Mariuccia Zerilli-Marimò's donation has established in perpetuity the Casa Italiana Zerilli-Marimò at New York University. The Joseph and Elda Coccia Institute for the Italian Experience in America is at Montclair State University. The Charles and Joan Alberto Italian Studies Institute (Seton Hall) and the Joseph M. and Geraldine C. La Motta Chair in Italian Studies are located at Seton Hall University. Also at Seton Hall U is the Valente Family Italian Studies Library (Seton Hall), a collection of Italian books second to none. On the west coast there is the George L. Graziadio Center for Italian Studies and its George L. Graziadio Chair of Italian Studies at California State University Long Beach. The Amelia V. Gallucci-Cirio Chair is at Fitchburg State College. On a different scale there is the Esposito Visiting Faculty Fellowship at UMass Dartmouth. Finally, the University of Central Florida has the Dr. Neil Euliano Chair in Italian Studies.

The majority of these programs include both Italian and Italian/American Studies as related fields of intellectual inquiry. To be sure, this is just the beginning. Italian/American Studies has progressed notably over the past thirty years at the college level. There are now a few programs or parts thereof nationwide at the undergraduate level. At the graduate level, instead, the situation is close to dire, to be sure. I would further contend that the more strident resistance comes from programs in Italian Studies, many of which still adhere to a canonical notion of what constitutes Italian Studies, or, as it is known in Italy, *italianistica*.

Indeed, for this to filter down to the public school system (where it is most needed in order to create future thinkers in this

---

[3] The other chairs sponsored entirely or in part by UNICO are located at the following universities: Seton Hall University (South Orange, NJ); Montclair State University (Montclair, NJ); California State University at Long Beach; Hofstra University (Hempstead, NY); State University of New York at Stony Brook.

regard), access to Italian/American Studies for more graduate students needs greater facilitation. This, simply, will not happen through public funding alone. There needs to be a significant articulation between the academic world and those of Italian America who can readily underwrite any and all of the above-mentioned entities, centers, and institutes. This includes graduate fellowships so that those in history, sociology, literature, cinema, and the like can dedicate themselves fulltime to earning their degrees, and not be distracted by having to work part-time. Because many of us have had to follow this second path, it does not mean our children and grandchildren should do the same. *Anzi!*

It is a great challenge that lies ahead, but it is surely a feasible accomplishment: The ten above-mentioned centers and professorships are proof positive. We thus need to talk, talk, and talk in order to do, do, and do…

The Francesco and Mary Giambelli Foundation now offers us an initial platform in which we can begin discussions among those of the greater population we call the Italian/American community. The Giambelli Foundation, to be sure, belongs to this small group of cultural philanthropists mentioned above. Indeed, because of its largesse, we at the John D. Calandra Italian American Institute were able to invite top scholars and intellectuals who have been negotiating this complex terrain we know as Italian America so that they may each in their own right launch various topics Italian Americans need to discuss first and foremost within the group to then be able to proceed to discuss such topics with other ethnic groups as well as with the hegemonic culture at large.

Fred Gardaphè is Distinguished Professor of English and Italian American Studies at Queens College CUNY. He has been instrumental in promoting and expanding the literary and cultural discipline of Italian/American Studies since the late 1980s. His essay in this book underscores the importance of education and the subsequent responsibilities that come with it as one converses with Italian Americana, especially if he/she has "made it." It is not enough to know the general history of Italian immigration to the United States. One must delve deep into said history, examining the various nooks and crannies, and come forth with a more nuanced discourse of how to move forward, especially for those who are in power positions in various Italian/American associations and NGOs.

Maria Laurino, in turn, is more of a public voice on the issue of Italian America. Her first two books fall into the category of memoir writing that brought to the surface the place of Italian Americans within the greater kaleidoscope that is the United States. While in her first book, the award-winning *Were You Always Italian?*,[4] she dealt with the overall notion of ethnic identity among Italian Americans, her second book, *Old World Daughter, New World Mother*,[5] as the title so clearly references, dealt with the gender issue and its conflicts with some old-world values that Italians brought with them to the United States. It is her third book that is the more general history of Italians in America. A companion piece to the PBS four-hour history of Italians in America,[6] Laurino's *The Italian American: A History*, is the latest in a line of histories.[7] In her article in this collection, Laurino draws comparisons with the Italian immigrants of yester-year and the current situation today of the how the United States has taken a more strident stance in identifying certain groups as undesirables.[8] This,

---

[4] See her, *Were You Always Italian?* (New York: Norton, 2000).
[5] See her, *Old World Daughter, New World Mother: An Education in Love and Freedom* (New York: Norton, 2009).
[6] John Maggio, dir. *The Italian Americans*. PBS, 2015. DVD.
[7] See her, *The Italian Americans: A History* (New York: Norton, 2014).
[8] For a similar notion, see my article, "When We Were the Muslims. President Trump's Executive Order and the Immigrant History of My Grandmother." *La Voce di New York*. January 29, 2017. https://www.lavocedinewyork.com/en/news/2017/01/29/when-we-were-the-muslims. The relevance of such notions of then and now

she adroitly demonstrates, is a repeat of what our own ancestors endured during the historical period of 1880-1924. In the end, she reminds us of the proverbial exhortation, "Lest we forget!"

World renown as a scholar of international migration, gender, and food studies, Professor Donna Gabaccia has authored and edited more than fifteen books on U.S. immigration, migration in world history, and the history of the Italian diaspora worldwide. In her more recent scholarship she has tackled more closely issues of interdisciplinarity and digital history. Her essay in this book explores the ways in which the "digital revolution of the past thirty years has ... changed the ways scholars ... understand Sambuca, a town of just under 6,000 residents located in the south western Sicilian province of Agrigento" (53). Indeed, as Professor Gabaccia continues in her study and ultimately demonstrates, a "close examination of digital archives on Sambuca ... reveals ... the unfulfilled potential of the digital revolution" (58), as it underscores some research already resolved and, at the same time, calls for the interrogation of new issues that would most readily come to the fore.

In his essay that closes this volume, "The Orphanage: Encounters in Transnational Space," Robert Viscusi examines a most significant issue, the historical relationship between Italians and Italian Americans. As something we never talk about but never forget, as Professor Viscusi states at the outset, this issue constitutes, as he writes, the "bitterest flavor of sibling rivalry, a condition where mutual distrust, envy, spite, and name-calling are endemic" (103). What Professor Viscusi does is study a century-long history (1891 to 1993) of the interactions between these two semiospheres, as we might call them, Italy and Italian America. Rightfully so, Professor Viscusi underscores the complexities of such a relationship that has seen, as he states herein:

---

and the interest in such comparisons is manifested by the fact that "When We Were the Muslims" has had more than 124,000 unique visitors and has had more than 24,000 shares.

> Migration historians tell us that 50% of the Italians who left during the years of the Great Migration (1880-1924) returned to Italy at least once, sometimes more than once. While the Fascist regime and the Second World War sharply interrupted this rhythm of return, the liberalization of U.S. immigration quotas in the 1950s primed the pump from Italy with relatively well educated migrants, and the economic progress of Italians outside Italy enabled them to engage in a new level of reconnection with the roots of their national culture and the branches of their families, towns, and provinces in the *madrepatria*. That their social ambitions should involve renewed involvement with a nation they had abandoned calls for some comment. (105-106)

This very relationship of a "renewed involvement with a nation they had abandoned" is wrought with a series of complexities and, to some degree, paradoxes, so that the "comment" that Professor Viscusi exhorts is something that will endure and develop for some time to come.

As I have mentioned above, much research has been done on socio-cultural Italian America within the past forty-plus years. What is encouraging is that in those very few — and I underscore *very few* — graduate programs where doctoral students are allowed to study Italian America and dedicate their dissertations to such subject matter, excellent research has come forth in the form of published essays and books. But we need much more! We need a strong and sustained commitment (*impegno*) to intellectualism that, to date, does not exist in any self-respecting manner. Gladly, we can state at this juncture, the Francesco and Mary Giambelli Foundation serves here as a model.

Essays

In Education Begin Responsibilities
Or, Why Italian Americans Don't Know What They Don't Know

FRED L. GARDAPHÉ

> *I have no child, I have nothing but a book,*
> *Nothing but that to prove your blood and mine.*
> William Butler Yeats, "Responsibilties"

DEDICATION

    This essay comes from inspiration I received at the last Giambelli Lecture by Robert Viscusi. I thank Foundation trustees Justine Tenney and Claudio DeVellis for suggesting the subject of education to me as I was telling them I would probably base my talk on humor and irony in Italian American culture, the book I've been working on for a while. Justine and Claudio helped me think back to the role education played in my life as an Italian American and how, since I've dedicated most of my life to learning about and teaching Italian American culture, I should have something to say about its past, present and future. And so I dedicate this essay to them and all who have helped me along the way of my own education, from my grandparents to the students in my classes today, for they have all taught me, in very different ways, that teaching others is the best way to learn about yourself. No one knows this better than the leader of this very Institute, Anthony Julian Tamburri, friend, colleague and the man who has helped me to turn many of my ideas into works, dreams into responsibilities, and responsibilities into action.

INTRODUCTION

    I take my title from two sources; the first and most obvious is a short story by Delmore Schwartz, a Jewish American Brooklyn born poet, who once, like me, studied at the University of Wisconsin. Born in 1913 he was considered one of the most gifted and promising young writers of his generation

Interrogations into Italian-American Studies
The Francesco and Mary Giambelli Foundation Lectures Series (2020)

Fred L. Gardaphé • "In Education Begins Responsibilities"

"In Dreams Begin Responsibilities," was published in 1937 in the very first issue of *The Partisan Review*. Schwartz took that title from the opening epigraph of a William Butler Yeats collection of poems entitled *Responsibilities* (1914). Yeats attributes his epigraph to something called *Old Play*, a reference whose origins have yet to be accurately ascertained.

In that poem, which ends with the lines of the epigraph I have attached, Yeats tells us that the things we wish to do with our lives are ours to choose, but beyond them, we are also responsible for those dreams we have, but never fulfill. In other words, it is our actions that dictate where our lives lead, and we cannot blame others for things we never accomplished. By not acting, or even trying to act, you just might be neglecting a responsibility, and without responsibilities dreams may never come true. Yeats is also saying that those who are older have much to teach, a responsibility to teach and to inspire the appetite for freedom, by telling the old stories that can ignite the dreams of youth.

Schwartz's story tells of an unnamed young man who has a dream that he is in an old-fashioned movie theater in 1909. As he sits down to watch, he realizes it's documenting his parents' courtship. The black-and-white silent film is of very poor quality, and the camera is shaky, but nonetheless he is engrossed. Soon the young man gets anxious. He yells things at the screen, as though he could affect the outcome of his parents' actions; other people in the audience begin to think he is crazy. Several times the character breaks down. In the end he shouts at his parents when it appears they are going to break up, forcing his eviction from the theater by an usher. In the end, the character wakes up from his dream and notes that it is the snowy morning of his twenty-first birthday. This story led the way to a number of stories and poems in which Schwartz emphasized the large divide that existed between his generation (which came of age during the Depression) and his parents' generation (who had often come to the United States as first-generation Jewish immigrants and whose idealistic view of America differed greatly from his own).

My subtitle comes from Lawrence DiStasi who when asked in

Will Parrinello's 1996 documentary, *Little Italy* why Italian Americans don't work to develop their culture, responded with, "They don't know what they don't know." It's a quote I use quite often as it has helped me understand why people will become defensive when they feel what they do know is being challenged, even when it isn't, and especially when they haven't been able to move beyond what they know. The current debate around Columbus is a good example of this.

In the space allotted to me I wish to merge these two quotes into a call for the support of the institutionalization of the study of Italian American culture, something that I have dedicated nearly my entire career to, a career that for sure has less days ahead than behind.

IL PASSATO: FARE L'AMERICA

Over forty years ago, the cries in Italian America were going out: "We've made it!" "There is no doubt at all that the Italians are moving very rapidly into the upper-middle class of American society," said Father Andrew Greely in an article appearing in the September/October 1973 issue of *Social Policy* entitled: "Making it in America: Ethnic Groups and Social Status." Ten years later, in "The Measure of Success," published in *Attenzione* magazine, Professor Richard Gambino, reinforced Greely's findings, basing his writing on a close analysis of the 1980 census. Gambino pointed to a gap in education:

> People of only Italian background have less education than other people of "pure" ethnic ancestry (28.6 percent of Italian males have completed at least one year of college, versus 36 percent of other single-ancestry males; the education gap between Italian females and other single-ancestry women is even greater. Still, the "pure" Italians do better than their lower education would lead us to expect. In fact, they have higher median family incomes than all the other single-ancestry people ($16,993 versus $15,764). In short, Italians of only Italian background have been able to overcome their educational handicap. (14)

This analysis led Gambino to say that for Italian Americans, "Education stands on the shoulders of money," unlike other ethnic groups whose "typical pattern of 'making it' has been to gain an education and use it to raise income" (15).

The rapid rise through class levels without the use of education is truly a phenomenon considering the background of America's seventh largest ethnic group. To understand how it was done, we need to know the stories of Italian immigration to the United States.

In his study, *The Social Background of the Italo-American School Child*, educator Leonard Covello gave us great insight as to why Italian Americans predominantly from the South of Italy, have traditionally avoided formal education:

> From the immigrant's point of view there was no obvious need for more than a trifling amount of formal education. All practical arts and skills should be acquired at an early age by working either in the parental household or though apprenticeship. Knowledge beyond the every-day requirements was a privilege and necessity for the "better" classes. (287)

For centuries Italy was rigidly divided into four social classes: the *giornaliero* or the day laborer; the *contadino* or peasant; the *borghese* or landowner; and the *galantuomini* or professionals.

The majority of Italians who emigrated to America came from the *giornaliero* and *contadino* classes, classes which for generations believed that one dies in the class he is born into and the sooner this is realized, the better life would be. Covello explains the *contadino*'s idea of education:

> In the first place, to the Italian parent, the idea of education or his concept of a person *buon educato* [a respectful, well mannered person] was remote from the concepts which served as a basis of school education, [which he termed as *buon instruito* or well instructed]. Formal education did not enter the sphere of his inter-

est. The wisdom of the group--the experience of generations and a projection of knowledge beyond that which is known—was transmitted through channels that were distinctly different from those of the school. (254)

Literacy was not a survival skill in the life of the *contadino*. To read the land and animal behavior was more important than the ability to read a book, which did little good in a land were books were rare.

The illiteracy rate of southern Italy was always among the highest in Europe. In 1901 the illiteracy rate of the South was reported to be: 70% in Campania, 70.9% in Sicily, 69.5% in Puglia, and 78.7% in Basilicata. Figures in regions of northern Italy at the same time showed from 32% to 46% illiteracy. A year later, a law was enacted that made school attendance compulsory for all children between the ages of six and nine years, yet by 1902 a study revealed that only 65% of the children between six and nine years were enrolled in the elementary schools (Covello 246).

What caused this?

Covello tells us "the school year was made in conformity to the climate and occupational conditions of northern Italy and in accordance with the cultural values of the northern Italy; it was never determined by the exigencies of southern regions (251). This resulted in neglect of governmental support for adequate educational facilities in the South and led to "Non-enforcement of compulsory education laws...promoted non only by the contadino class, but by the upper class and the clergy who were antagonistic to education for the peasant. (274), a situation not unlike the negative attitudes attached to those who might educate slaves in the U.S.

And so we find that formal education was seen more as a threat to the order of the family. Any benefit that formal education could provide the individual would be far outweighed by the trouble it would cause the family.

Covello reported that:

> To the *contadino* parent, education was the handing down of all the cultural, social and moral value of his society through the medium of folklore, or the teaching, generation after generation, of the child by the parents. The peasant's desire for security in his way of living was directly opposed to education from outside the family circle" (403).

Inadequate facilities, poor instruction and information found to be of little practical value to the children of the *contadini,* combined to keep formal education in a negative light; it simply did not fit into the demands of the family's struggle for survival.

There is a saying in southern Italy: "Fesso chi fa il figlio meglio di lui," "It is a fool who makes his child better than himself." Author Helen Barolini explains this well in her "Introduction" to *The Dream Book.* "In America, schools were not always regarded as the road to a better future; more often they were seen as a threat to the family because they stressed assimilation into American ways.... Learning gave one ideas, made one different; all the family wanted was cohesion" (8).

DRAMATIC INTERLUDE

What follows is the account of Moustache Pete, a character I created from the Chicago Oral History project directed by Dominic Candeloro and from the many interviews I conducted with first-generation immigrants in my early years as a journalist for the *Fra Noi* news. Pete's experiences dramatize some of the issues faced by immigrants regarding education in Italy and the U.S.A.

SIX: SEPTEMBER, 1985

When I wasa grow up in Italy I wen' a school, maybe two days. School in my land start right when was harvest time. The first day of school, boy I was so happy to think I would get out of work, but I shoulda know better. Right when we get to the story about the Romans, my father come an knock down the door. He say he need me in the fields. So he pull me right out of the school. The other day was so cold in the school that everbuddy sit on they hands and listen to the teach until they fall sleep. That was my time in school.

You see back in the old country nobuddy need a school. An they was no girls in our school back then. I doan know, could be the ladies think if you teach your daughter to read and write then she goan write love letters to some stranger. Wasn't too many boys in our school either. What could school teach that the old timers couldn't tell us. Was no school to tell us how to milk a goat or bake bread or how to make the garden grow. You wan learn how to do somethin you go to someone who does it and work with them. That's how you learn back then.

But when we come to 'merica was a different story. All of sudden was so important to go to school. I never did go to school, but cause I didn't wanna be un-American I send my kids to school. I tell you I doan think it did my kids any good. Oh, doan get me wrong, they got the good educaysh. Some got degrees in medicine an' law an some even become the teach. But you know somethin, I wonder joosta how smart they are iffa they gotta watch televish to find out if goan rain or snow.

One time my boy he call me up and say pop, better put you storm windows up, soon is gonna snow. I tell him he's crazy. I can smell when a snow is comin and is no where near. Is gonna be one more warm stretch I tell him. But you think he listen to me? No. So when the Indian summer come along he can't breath in his house cause he got it already all locked up for winter. That's what his fancy educaysh got him, a stuffy house.

I tell you I think the more people go to school the dumber they get. They get so they can no depend on they own common sense no more. They buy junk inna store, stead of raisin' they own food inna garden; why pay good money for somethin you can have for a little hard work and some grace of God. Trouble with this country is too much educaysh. Why even got it on the televish. They's people who talk to the televish and never to they family. The kids move far away from they family to find a better life an' they talk family bizness onna phone stead of face to face.

Now you tell me, "Eh Pete, that's what you did. You leave Italy to come here." But I tell you when I leave Italy was because they was no chance to make a good life there. But here, in America you can make a good life right next door to you family, just as good as goin thousand miles away. I break up my family in Italy so that I can make it better one day for my own family. But now my family is spread out all round this big country.

I doan know what is gonna happen to all those people with book smarts. I think sometimes they gotta read so much because they forget how to read life with they own eyes and ears. They get so they always need advice from some expert before they can do something simple. What's wrong with just talkin, talkin and listenin' that was what educaysh in my day. My father talk and I listen. But come ci fa? What you goan do? Is a whole new world since they drop the bomb, eh?

MANNAGGIA L'AMERICA

For his study Covello interviewed hundreds of first-generation Italian Americans. The following excerpt points to a situation common to most Italian immigrants:

> "Before I sailed to America our local priest attempted to scare us by telling about the difficulty of learning English. But we knew better; we knew that there would be no need to torture oneself with a strange language... When I arrived in New York I went to live with my *paesani*. I did not see any reason for learning English. I didn't need it, for everywhere I lived or worked or fooled around there were only Italians... I had to learn some Sicilian, though, for I married a girl from the province. Sicilian helped me a great deal in my family and in my work... I don't speak much English, but that never bothered me." (279)

How true this is to those of us whose relatives once lived in the many Little Italies throughout the United States. So what happened when immigrant families arrived in a land where education was considered to be a means of upward mobility? Again we turn to

Covello for an answer:

> The retention of Italian family mores and patterns led to an attempt to impose these patterns upon the American scene. Since the education of children in southern Italy was carried on mainly in the home, within the inclusive environment of the traditional *contadino* family organization, compulsory school attendance in America led to antagonism and conflict between the *contadino* family and the school. (328)

Covello illustrates this point with an anecdote taken from an oral interview:

> "Most people believe that Italians came here mainly for economic reasons. But it is erroneous to overlook that in America they sought to find freedom from various deviltries of the Italian government. Among these were the attempts to introduce compulsory education, which the peasant in southern Italy considered more of a burden than a blessing. So when here in America he was confronted with compulsion to send his children to school, regardless of sex, age or the financial background of the home, he showed a tendency to resist, especially when this compulsion was accompanied by the fear that the children might be imbued by the school with ideas antagonistic to the traditions of the parents... If they sent them to school at all, they did so because they did not want to appear as barbarians" (288).

Covello himself was an immigrant and came to America with his family in 1894. He devoted his whole life to improving the educational system not only for Italian immigrants but for all immigrants. In his memoir, *The Heart is the Teacher*, written along with novelist Guido D'Agostino, he relates a story that is representative of the second generation's experience with the American educational system, and perhaps the most quoted excerpt of his work:

> During this period [1900s] the Italian language was completely ignored. In fact throughout my whole elementary school career, I do

not recall one mention of Italy or the Italian language or what famous Italians had done in the world, with the possible exception of Columbus, who was pretty popular in America. We soon got the idea that Italian meant something inferior and a barrier was erected between children of Italian origin and their parents. This was the accepted process of Americanization. We were becoming Americans by learning how to be ashamed of our parents (43).

The following anecdote comes from Covello's interviews and illustrates this shame:

"In my early years we were highly critical if not disrespectful of the many traditions that the old folks wanted us to live up to and conform to. We were tired of hearing about how good the old town in Italy was. Many of my Italian friends would say, 'They have lived their own lives in their own way. We want to live our lives in our own way and not be tied down to fantastic customs that appear ridiculous not only to us but particularly to our 'American' friends. And I can assure you we were particularly keen about that ridicule. In fact so much so that we never invited our 'American' 'friends' to our home. And while American boys took their parents to some of the school functions, we not only did not take our parents, but never even told them they were taking place. That was our life--exclusively ours and that of the other boys. The deadline was the threshold of the house or the tenement in which we lived. Beyond that the older folks went their way and we went ours'" (340).

Children of the immigrants entering American schools faced the problem of dealing with not one, but two cultures. Often, what the child learned in school challenged what he had learned in the home, as in these examples provided by Covello:

"'Lunch at elementary school was a difficult problem for me. To have a bite I either stole some money from home or took it from my shoe shining on Saturdays and Sundays.

With this money I would buy the same stuff that non-Italian boys were eating. To be sure, my mother gave me each day an Italian sandwich, that is a loaf of French bread filled with fried peppers and onions, or one half dipped into oil and some minced garlic on it. Such a sandwich would certainly ruin my reputation; I could not take it to school... My God, what a problem it was to dispose of it, for I was taught never to throw away bread...'" (339).

"At elementary school I was thrilled with everything that was taught about America; its history, geography, and what it stands for. It was very pleasant to hear about it. But when I came home in the afternoon, I felt a painful contrast between what I saw at home and what had been taught during the day. The teacher had said, for instance, that clean hands, clean clothing and a toothbrush are essentials. And that plenty of milk should be taken in the morning. I felt so ashamed, so inferior, when I realized that my parents do not exemplify such things at home. My mother showed even opposition to the teacher's recommendation about food. She began ridiculing my teachers for their ideas, and this made me very sad, for she ruined my dreams of becoming a real American.

"I felt that I needed milk in the morning more than anything else. But my mother, and so my father, insisted that this was not according to the good customs; that American milk was poison. 'These teachers of yours are driving us crazy,' they told me. I realized that everything I learned at school was met by my parents with disapproval. So I did not bring up such things any more for I did not want to be accused of being a disobedient son and cause trouble between myself and my other relatives. The family came first.... (341).

A parent explains why this is important:

"The American school is bad, very bad. They teach a lot of things that don't help nobody. You have got to educate first and then the child will learn. A child who is *educato* will learn. He will learn easily because he is obedient, has respect for parents, has good manners. He is home with is family. He has *buona educazione* and *educazione* must always come before *istruzione*. The family, of course, must give *educazione* but the school must do it too. The school does not do it." (325)

Sometimes this dilemma led to behavior or learning problems in school. "'As soon as I entered this school where there were few Italian kids, I got the idea that I was not as good as other people. I felt very inferior to the other fellows--I was afraid to get up and speak in class and consequently it showed its effect on my work, and I was on the verge of quitting school'" (344).

The tensions created by the pressures of assimilation led to the creation of a gap between the "American" child and the Italian parent. So it seems that a child could survive by outwardly rejecting the culture of his family while inwardly clinging to the culture he had been raised in. This dilemma accounts for the second generation's inability to communicate in Italian, while insisting that their children abide by customs and rules that have been inherited from the first generation. This, and the fact that Italy declared war on the United States in 1941, helps us to understand why Italian Americans know little about their own history and the culture of their ancestors. Such knowledge had little to do with becoming American and certainly was not something that was taught in the schools. Italian Americans go through life, not knowing what they don't know, relying on what they do know to make their decisions. This move to assimilate would lead Italian Americans to "rootlessness".

The Italian Americans who grew up during the Great Depression learned from an early age the value of hard work and simple lifestyles were the only ways to get ahead. Many carried on family businesses or took advantage of the Post War Industrial boom to find good steady work. The first big surge in Italian Americans pursuing higher education occurred just after the end of World War II, when many veterans took advantage of the G.I. Bill. But it is the children of these veterans who sought higher education in even greater numbers. In his 1983 article, "Measure of Success,"

Fred L. Gardaphé • "In Education Begins Responsibilities"

Richard Gambino wrote:

> The work ethic of 'l'ordine della famiglia' finally paid off in the decades that followed the peaking of Italian immigration in 1907. Each generation raised its children economically on its shoulders through patterns of hard work, savings, investment in and improvement of real property and family businesses. It is only now, securely in the middle class, that Italian Americans of single ancestry feel they can afford the 'luxury' of sending their children to college. And not without some misgivings about schools loosening traditional family values in their children. (15)

Gambino goes on to state that as the work ethic changes so does the "family order." The result he predicts is a weakening of the family. Anyone who has a brother or sister who has gone off to college then moved away from home can relate to this. In my experience, while growing up, no matter where I turned there was family: an uncle to teach me how to hike a football, an aunt to babysit, a cousin to play with. It was different for my son and daughter. For them it's was a half-hour ride to nonna's house and a three hour flight to their cousins in Florida. Was it education that did this to our family? Is it what my family taught me that makes me miss the closeness? An old saying goes you can't make wine and jam from the same grapes. You've got to chose one or the other. And it seems that you can't be "buon educato" and "buon istruito" at the same time, or can you?

IL PRESENTE: FROM THE STREETS INTO ACADEMIA

In 1980 the Agnelli Foundation published a study that used statistics gathered by Fr. Andrew Greeley with the National Opinion Research Institute. The study concluded:

> [T]he high rate of mobility already recorded makes it quite probable that this group will be making enormous advances in the immediate future. Of course, if we combine the quantitative data with qualitative suggestions (we already know about the tendency on

the part of Italian Americans to attend medium rather than top-rated or Ivy League schools, to major in engineering rather than in the arts or sciences, to terminate their education before they reach the highest academic degree-the PhD- and not to opt for an academic career), we can demonstrate that the extremely pragmatic attitude displayed by Italian Americans in choosing careers and the weight they give the income factor in that choice carries over into educational decisions. We should not therefore expect as massive an Italian presence in the academic world as the Jewish American or WASP presence—at least not any time soon. What we can expect, though, is a healthily irreverent utilization of education as a channel for upward social mobility, a view of education as a tool, rather than as 'end use'." (22)

Such statistics suggest that Italian Americans would continue to rise in education as well as income, but what further effects would such education have on the family and would they still refer to themselves as Italian American?

The American Commissioner of Labor reported that during the last decade of the 19th Century, approximately one-third of all Italians in the four largest cities in the country were living in poverty. Today, as we near the end of the 20th Century, that poverty is barely a memory. Italian Americans have surpassed the nation's median income and statistics suggest that the upward mobility that we have been experiencing is continuing.

The rapid economic growth of the nation's once second largest immigrant group, which today is the nation's seventh largest ethnic group can be attributed to the Italian Americans' belief that hard work and a stringent savings program was the way to succeed. However, until recently, this success has been based on well-paying jobs as opposed to well-planned careers. A brief review of the work history of Italian Americans will help us to understand this.

According to a 1911 U.S. Immigration report to the Senate, of the almost two million southern Italian immigrants who had come to the United States between 1899 and 1910, less than one half of one percent were in the professions and only 15% were in skilled occupations. 77% were farm workers or laborers. These immigrants came to work and worked wherever they could find employers who could use unskilled and illiterate manpower. That meant the majority broke their backs as common laborers on construction projects. This group included many who came to this country with skills that could not be practiced due to discrimination, an inability to overcome the language barrier or low demand for the trade.

The thought of a career would rarely come to a man whose major concern was survival. One could not sit back and decide on a career to pursue and then take the time to secure the proper training needed for a career. Work was a practical solution to the reality of poverty. And job, not career, was the only available remedy. This attitude was passed on from the first generation to the second and, for the most part, carried on.

"As recently as 1950," wrote Professor Rudolph Vecoli in 1976, "the occupational structure of the Italian Americans continued to be one of a broad base of blue collar workers with a much thinner strata of professions, businessmen and white-collar employees. Among the first generation there was a strong persistence in the manual occupations and a definite underrepresentation in the higher status occupations, white the occupational profile of the second generation continued to bear a striking resemblance to that of their immigrant parents" (2).

It was a major concern for Italian Americans to seek out work that paid well rather than to find work that carried with it high prestige. However, statistics do point to a transition from low-prestige, low-income occupations to better ones at better pay. Based on statistics compiled by Richard Gambino in 1975 and published by the Agnelli Foundation in its study of Italian Americans, breaks these statistics down into upper, middle and working class (for men only):

	1950	1970
Upper Classes	16%	28%
Middle Classes	36%	32%
Lower Classes	46.7%	33%

These tables do not take into consideration the numbers of third and fourth generation Italian Americans, who were more likely to have used the American educational system as a means for upward mobility. Thus the difference between the first and second generation Italian Americans in terms of upward mobility is not as great as we will find between the second and third generation.

In a 1976 article on Italian Americans, Rudolph Vecoli wrote:

> In a 1969 survey of major corporations by ethnic origin, the Italian males were only slightly underrepresented among professional and technical workers as compared with the total population. They also lagged somewhat behind all other groups (except Spanish) as managers, officers and proprietors; but they led in the category of clerical workers. The proletarian heritage of the Italians was reflected in their strong showing as craftsmen, foremen, ranking second only to Poles. Again, as operatives and laborers, they were second only to the Spanish" (48).

This finding followed and substantiated Andrew Greely's article in *Social Policy*, 1973 entitled, "Making it in America: Ethnic Groups and Social Status":

> In the era between 1950 and 1970, then, the Catholic ethnic groups, with the possible exception of the Poles, moved from the lower-middle class and working class into the upper-middle class. Not all of their members, of course, enrolled in the white-collar world, but they were as likely to be in that world--and in most cases, more likely--than the American average" (29).

For Italian Americans, this means that the third generation carried the group's status upward. The 1980 Census figures on the occupations of Americans who were of Italian ancestry were reported in the breakdown for males and females, according to occupations is as follows:

Managerial	25.7	Farming	1.3
Technical	33.5	Precision	10.4
Service	13.9	Operative	15.2

These figures reflected the participation of third and fourth generation Italian Americans and suggest that education and career orientation have worked to improve the position of Italian Americans in the labor force.

The 1980 Census figures according to income showed us a different class break down for Italian Americans.

Upper Class	36.8
Middle Class	42.1
Lower Class	21.1

Let's take a look at a number of factors that contributed to this rapid social mobility. The American economy at the time of the great Italian immigration was an industrial based economy. Such an economy naturally required the muscle of blue collar workers. Because work and income directly benefited the family, first generation Italian Americans started with whatever jobs they could get and then slowly but surely moved on to jobs that paid better once they acquired skills that enabled them to do so.

By nature, blue-collar workers have a stronger group consciousness, as they more often than not worked in and with groups. This consciousness led to strong Italian American participation in the union movement. Unions would enable these workers to preserve the security of their jobs and consequently, the integrity of the family. As the financial position of this generation improved and their children came along, they impressed upon their offspring the need to work industriously in order to succeed. Laziness was not tolerated and in fact brought shame. As soon as children were able to work, they were put to work in the home and often as apprentice workers when the father, uncle, godfather or friend could find a position.

Those growing up during the Great Depression learned quickly that the only way to make it in America was to have work, quite often that then meant two or three part-time jobs when a full-time job could not be found. This early work consciousness and emphasis on financial survival of the family eschewed the luxury of planning for the future. It was only as the second generation matured, during the Second World War, that we find the movement from focus on the well paying job, to the well planned career.

As the economy shifted in the 1950s and 60s from an industrial to a technological based economy, muscle was less in demand as brains were required to handle the technological advances in industry. For the first time, educational benefits were extended to war veterans, yet, the majority of Italian American war veterans, returned to the work force instead of studying for careers. The careers, they would rationalize, could belong to their children if they could provide them with the opportunity to pursue an education.

As I prepared this article, I talked to a number of people of the second and third generation who were able to establish and reach career goals. One lawyer, who asked to remain anonymous, told me that his career was chosen for him. "When I finished high school, I was thinking of going to work. There were things I wanted, like a car and spending money. My father showed me his calloused hands and told me that this was what happened to the man who works for a boss. It was then when he told me that I was going to college and then to law school. When I told him I thought we couldn't afford it. He said, 'You worry about the books and let me worry for the affording.' Of course, I'm happy now that I became a lawyer, but to do so I had to abandon hopes of deciding on my own career. I don't know what I would have become if I had been able to make my own decisions. My family had to sacrifice for seven years to help me through school, but they never once griped."

A doctor told me that his family pushed him into medical school because the largest family expense at that time was medical bills. He jokingly added, "I'm happy that most of our money wasn't going to food, then I'd probably have been told to go into the grocery business."

This is a pattern that many Italian Americans have in common. They were afforded the luxury of an education, but not the choice of what they would study. They tended to choose careers that brought high incomes, especially careers in law, medicine and business. "Education was only good if it kept you from doing what your parents did. My father said, 'I have a good job, but you are going to have something that don't depend on someone else for a raise,'" said an investment broker. "My father said, 'I use my back, you use your brains. So when you're old like me your back won't be bent.'"

So while Italian Americans have successfully shifted from a blue collar to a white based ethnic group, the question that arises is how has this shift affected their ethnicity and the major source of Italian American identity: the family?

First generation Italian Americans came from larger families necessitated by the agrarian society they were born into. Large families were needed to form the production team. Second generation Italian Americans were, for the most part, born into smaller families as the new industrialized economy no longer required entire family participation for financial survival. Third generation and fourth generation Italian Americans were born into still smaller families with the improvement in economic well-being and the advent of family planning. Material success enables greater freedom in terms of travel both within one's birthplace and outside of it: money for cars, for vacations. As Italian Americans moved from blue collar to white-collar work, they also changed habitats: from inner city to suburban life. Families, more often than not, moved out of city neighborhoods as nuclear families. Relationships outside of the ethnic group and the family group soon developed to replace those that had primarily been intra-family and intra-ethnic. Gone are the days of daily contact with extended family members in the neighborhood, workplace, school or market. Now such interaction is almost entirely restricted to family affairs such as weddings, funerals and birthdays.

Friendships among Italian Americans over the generations have moved beyond those of immigrants who primarily socialized with other Italians. As one moves up the levels of society, via education and career, contact with members of other ethnic groups of similar class status increases and friendships develop more along class lines than through any shared ethnicity. Thus, Italian Americans are more likely to identify with their particular social class than with their ethnic heritage.

During the 1980s I spent much time studying the many cultures that make up the USA. I had studied African American, Jewish American, Irish American, Asian American, Hispanic American, and was wondering, as does Spike Lee's character Buggin' Out in the film *Do the Right Thing*, where were the pictures of *my* people on the walls of the local institutions. That's when I decided to focus my time and energy on Italian American studies.

Throughout all my studies I learned much, but nothing more important than what I learned about two different nations and what happened when one migrated to the other. These were some of the most important lessons I ever learned in or out of school, and it prepared me to devote my life to developing Italian and American studies in the context of American studies.

I did this outside of school with the hopes that if I worked hard enough future generations would be able to do this within their education. Good education is always about revolution, and it will continue to be. But the real revolution comes when the head turns in new and different directions. Students need to learn about all the cultures that are part of their country; whether it is through textbooks or other resources we need to be reminded that this country was founded on the principle of resistance to economic, social and political tyranny, while at the same time enabling humans to dream and work to make those dreams come true.

When I created my first course in Italian American culture, nearly forty years ago I had very little to work with in terms of syllabi, lesson plans and models of teaching. I worked with the research that had been produced, primarily by members of the American Italian Historical Association, and a few other scholars of the Italian Amerian experience. I can remember thinking, in the middle of some of my lectures, that I was literally making this all up, for these were ideas I had never been taught in all my many years of education from kindergarten through graduate school. The only models I had were those that were being created through the multicultural education movement that was taking place at the time, and they came in handy for structuring courses and lessons.

The greatest problem I encountered in those early classes came from the very students I had most hoped to reach: those descendants of Italian immigrants.

Italian American students were afraid of taking my courses. Why? Perhaps they didn't want to sign up for something that would make them look like a minority; perhaps they feared looking ignorant about something they assumed they should already know. What they didn't know, at the time, was that it was something in their very own culture that contributed to this feeling of inferiority, and that was *bella figura*. Not wanting to look bad in class, something most students fear, was quite *brutta* for those Italian American students. Ignorance, a literal not knowing, from the Ancient Greek "I gnosis," I've found, is the basis for almost every fear we can have.

And there was more, so much more: they didn't know that they had come from a culture of indirection, which avoids direct public confrontation by using intermediary actions and people to communicate what they will allow others to know about themselves. But something great happened when these students came to understand the underpinnings of their culture. For one, they learned the meaning of the *parolacce* or bad words that they had no trouble using with good effect at the right times without a clue as to what they were actually saying. They understood the rationale behind the gold jewelry they often wore in the shape of horns. They could finally answer the question why their family had emigrated from Italy, if not yet where exactly they had lived in the old country. They began to understand things about their family like never before. Many would go home to their families and tell them what they learned in school, and by the time I was teaching at Stony Brook, many of them asked if their family members could come to visit the classes. When they began finding out what they had never known before, they began wanting to explore Italy more. Many decided to start studying Italian, and my classes became the back door for Italian language courses that had seen dwindling enrollments, and this led to an increased demand for Italian language courses.

Now what I was teaching, and the effect my courses were having were just a drop in the bucket of what was needed in the U.S., especially considering the way Italian American culture was being presented to the world on television and through the organizations that acted as spokesmen for the culture. It took years of hard work for American scholars of Italian descent to convince American academics that Italian American studies was a valid field of inquiry, and even more years for it to be accepted as a valuable addition to educational programs. Yet, in spite of the successes, there is a long way to go.

IL FUTURO: OUR RESPONSIBLITIES TO LEAD FORWARD

The experience of Italian immigration to the United States can help us explore the effects of globalization on the identity of Italians; for Italian immigrants to the United States were put into the position of constantly negotiating their relationship between their local culture of origin and their local culture of they land of immigration. Because of this process, Italian Americans have begun to grow into a more glocal people. The adoption of the English Language, and the refusal to maintain Italian gives us a glimpse as to what is the difference between Italianità and what Professor Piero Basetti has coined "Italicità." This renunciation of the national experience, of Italian immigrants, involved the process of emigration, immigration, and the formation of Little Italy. The creation of Italian America was a defensive reaction that helped protect the vulnerable Italian immigrant through the replanting process. As the Italian moved away from the little Italys, the risks and the rewards became greater. For example, many immigrant men received U.S. citizenship by fighting in the various wars.

The interaction between global and local often took place in schools, sometimes even in homes through mass media. The Italian American learned early not to depend on a single master narrative to explain national identity; for U.S. identity was the results of the syntheses of competing narratives that individuals are exposed to. Thus, we see Italian American identity being formed out of both history and story. Until recently there has been a film/fiction emphasis in Italian American culture, vs. non-fictional via documentary studies. When we begin to examine just what it is that can be called Italian American culture, we see that Italianità becomes a closet with all the claustrophobia that small spaces encourage. Rarely is there an horizon in an Italian American film, novel. Even the paintings by Italian Americans tend toward the urban, the crowded and closed up as opposed to possible meditations on the open spaces of the country and the unknown, the natural. Instead, there is a claustrophobic concentration on the known, the familiar, as though reality and history were a mantra that could make everything safe if simply repeated often enough.

Where the local identities are strong is where Italian Americans are an integral part of political and social infrastructure; where it is weak is where there's little or no connection to that community. Italian Americans were cut from nation before Italy had created a strong sense of national identity. This experience facilitates the movement away from *Italianità* and toward *Italicità*.

The idea of a glocal identity requires the possibility of acknowledging multiple identities. This can best take place if we first acknowledge it in ourselves, and then understand and acknowledge it in others. This is why is it so important for Italian Americans to understand their own histories. The problem, if this does not occur, is that Italian Americans will become fixed on how others identify them: as gangsters, buffoons, obsessed with food, etc., and the other ways society packages and consumes commodities inspired by Italian culture. While much of this representation and commodification is simply so much spice to create alternatives to the bland, Anglo-Saxon fare, it is also a way to project opposites to a people obsessed with separating good and evil, light and dark, black and white.

Without knowledge of ethno-history, without knowledge of ethno-stories, Individual ethnic groups are limited to reacting to what others produce, and are thus kept from creating their own expressions. Italian Americans are being defined by others and not by themselves.

Italian Americans have been like the character in the Delmore Schwartz story. Confronting the past of their ancestors can drive people crazy because they realize that their present was the ancestors' future, and this knowledge creates the reality that the responsibility for the future is now theirs.

For any Italian American who has examined his or her physical and mental state, it is no surprise that there is indeed a great deal of difference visible when we begin comparing generations. Yet some things do move through generations unchanged and we tend to refer to these characteristics as our heritage. However, beyond the packaged products, costumes, and food, heritage is composed of processes, ways of being, ways of behaving.

Typically these products and processes move from generation to generation by way of elders, both in their words and their actions. I still can't stand to see food wasted, and have often avoided ordering a full meal in a restaurant when I'm with my children. This is something I learned from my grandparents and parents. It is often looked upon as crude behavior, but the *scarpetta*, using a bit of bread to gather up gravies on my plate was something expected by my family, but frowned upon the first time I ate in a non-Italian home. My sister is really the true keeper of this tradition in our family; she can turn a fried chicken leg into a piece of bony pipe. This waste-not, want not attitude is one of those physical products of our heritage.

In terms of processes, the stories of our past, especially when told by our elders, has been the major vehicle by which our heritage is transmitted from generation to generation. But this process became endangered when Italians migrated to America. Loss of shared primary languages, lack of shared environments (as children leave not only the homes, but the neighborhoods and often the states of their upbringing), contributed to the distorted transmission of our heritage. This unconscious is rarely addressed in the gangster films of our talented, film and video directors who are more likely to be interested in making money by following a formula guaranteed to bring in money at the expense of repressing if not outright avoiding and sometimes denying the truth.

Education is about the interplay between the known and the unknown. There is a tension created between the conscious and the unconscious of the Italian American people. By conscious, I mean the ways we identify ourselves as Italian Americans and the ways we express that identity. By unconscious, I mean the psychic elements that haunt us in our private thoughts, that come to us in dreams that we cannot tell anyone about, those thoughts and feelings that we cannot understand unless we engage in some type of counseling. I am generalizing to make a point, not to point a finger, so please bear with me on this. As Italian Americans move up the economic ladder of success, they are doing so at the risk of losing their very identity as Italian Americans.

At the end of a section of her novel, *Umbertina*, Helen Barolini has the matriarch of a family sitting by her self near a tree during a family reunion picnic. She looks around and is proud of what she and her husband created out of the nothing that they brought with them to America. But then, there is a sadness that overcomes her to the point of tears, and that is when she comes to realize that of all the relatives here, there is no one to whom she can tell her story. Not one of her daughters or sons, granddaughters or grandsons, can nor will they ever know her story:

> She had won, but who could she tell her story to? At times the doubt came to her whether she had really won, after all. All her life had been a struggle for family, and now in her old age she saw some signs that made her uneasy.... (145).

It is not long before this uneasiness, becomes a dis-ease of sorts, and many of you know that it is not simply the stuff of novels. This occurs in every family in which the experience of one generation was denied entry into the consciousness of the next. More often then than not, this occurred when the language of the immigrants was not passed on to their children.

Fred L. Gardaphé • "In Education Begins Responsibilities"

Remember, the immigrants' experiences were processed in Italian, and were they not recorded, not passed on from one generation to the next, it mostly like was due to the impossibility of communicating such complex thoughts and feelings in a new language. By the time I learned to speak, read, and write Italian, my grandparents were dead and my parents had stopped speaking the language. What was lost only I could imagine, so I went in search of those stories. What I found was that while they couldn't control how they passed down a heritage through conscious stories, they did pass down some unconscious elements that we must understand before we can succeed as a culture. One of those elements is the idea of captivity.

Whatever Italy is to you, whatever it has become since World War II, its people have yet to deal with the impact on the individual psyche caused by centuries of rule by invaders. Italians notions of *figura*, of *sprezzatura*, of putting on a front, of not letting people know what you really think and feel, is the result of living amidst the enemy. You don't need to be a psychiatrist to realize that to live this life requires the construction of two or more selves; this is nothing particularly Italian, it something that happens whenever a person is held in captivity or slavery.

This psychic defense of splitting the self that serves from the self that rebels is something that we have inherited whether we understand it or not. Some have referred to it as immigrant fear, but it goes back long before immigration. This feeling of being two selves of has translated into a sense of being Italian and American, and it is a feeling that has rarely been recognized, and only recently is it being dealt with in mental health studies and practices. However, it has always been there in our stories. We need to understand more how this psychic defense of splitting has resulted in the punishment and reward systems used in our families, we need to understand how this splitting impacts our lives today when we no longer live in physical captivity yet maintain the psychic defenses to it and continue to use it. It is part of what Freud has called our emotional heritage. This is what I mean when I talk about understanding the Italian/American unconscious, and a good place to start is with our stories.

The work of Italian American intellectuals, while in many ways the avant-garde of Italian American culture, has not been a strong part of Italian American identity, yet. The very members of our community who call themselves leaders have not done enough to educate, or lead Italian Americans forward, mostly because they haven't taken the time to study the great work that has been done in the field.

Now that we are developing Italian American studies at all levels of education, Italian American culture will become part of the American educational system in ways unimaginable by previous generations. What is called for is nothing less than to include Italian American histories and stories in the body of material that one must master to be considered American. Even Italians have not paid adequate attention to Italian American thought and culture, sometimes seeing in it a mirror of its own weaknesses, its own past, refusing to see how some people chose to answer that infamous "*Questione Meridionale*," the Southern Question that never seems to go away. The vital familism of Italian American culture has permeated American culture through the work of artists such as Francesco Capra, a Sicilian immigrant who defined America through the power of his films which have touched many generations. This also comes into play in such strange places as HBO's *The Sopranos*, in which an Italian American producer-director redefined what it means to be a citizen of the United States in a post millennium culture.

Before we can understand all of this, we must become familiar with the way that Italian Americans have been defined and redefined since the arrival of the first Italian immigrants to the United States. What is needed is nothing less than ethnic reinvention, something, Michael M. J. Fischer tells us, is accomplished through a narrative's "inter-references between two or more cultural traditions" which "create reservoirs for renewing humane values" (201). By identifying and reading these inter-references we will be able to see that, as Fischer concludes, "Ethnic memory is ... or ought to be future, not past oriented" (201).

The key to creating a future for Italian/American culture that means something to today's youth is to first insure that they have access to histories, of their families and of their communities, then we must provide them with historical and contemporary models in the areas of arts, business, and education, that they can study, emulate and transcend. We have created scholarships for higher education, but we have done little to help those applicants understand what it means to be Italian American once they enter those institutions. Italian Americans need to understand the value of creating new knowledge, they need to trust intellectual pursuits; all this is the responsibility of those who can, of those who care, of those who knows what needs to be done.

Yeats called on his elders to face their responsibilities of leading forward through example, through support of what they consider to be worthwhile, through education. I ask the same of all of you. What have you done, what can and what will you do to "prove your blood" to the next generations?

DRAMATIC FINALE

I couldn't leave you without a little more drama, and so what follows is the last two segments of Moustache Pete's story of how he once tried adult education. I leave you with the Pete's words because they reflect the frustrations faced and the struggles that immigrant ancestors went through in their attempts to *fare la merica*.

TWENTY-TWO: MARCH 1987

"Chi va a scuola dell'obbligo, sempre viaggia solo." That's a old time saying that means, "Whoever goes to forced school will always travel alone."

Now I used to think I know what this means. Back when I wasa grown up only was a few kids, mostly the sick kids, who go to obligatory school. And they never had many friends cause was only a few of them in school. So it was like they was goin on a voyage by themselves.

Fred L. Gardaphé • "In Education Begins Responsibilities"

Until joosta few weeks ago I never did spend much time in shcool. In fact, the last time I was in school was over sixty years back and that was for joosta few days. So now that old Pete is back in school I fine myself lookin back on all I learned in life and I begin to think twice about it all. Like with these proverbs.

Those were words that educated us. None of us used to believe that going to school had anything to do with life. Back then school was joost for peple who could afford the time to sit and learn to read. And in those days they wasn't so much to read. So school wasa biga waste of time. And when the governo di Italia tell us all we have to go to school my father put his foot down. He say, "If they goan try to take my kids away from me then, I'm goan take my kids away from them." And so that's when we moved out of the town and onto the land.

When I come to this country wasa big surprise for me when the government tell me the say thing, you gotta send you kids to school. Now I wasa so mad that at first I was goan tell the governo that we didn't have no kids, but because he live such a different life here, they was nothing for my kids to do. Stay at home, play in the streets or go to school. So my wife she beg me, "Please Pietro, let you kids go to school. They joosta goan get in trouble if you don't."

So I give in and send them all to school. But they they come back from school and tell me they goan stop to speak Italian, I wasa so mad. "Who are they to tell my kids they can no speak they own language?" I was so mad I march down to the school and was ready for a big fight. Now back then I didn't speak sucha good English like I do now. So when I meet the teach was no way for me to tell her what I think. I had to go back home and bring my oldest boy for me to translate.

Now have you ever had to argue through a translator? I'm tellin you it's not the same. You got to wait for something to yell at and then wait again for your words to fight back. It's no fun to fight that way. Is too much building up steam and lettin it seep out instead of to explode. That's when I decided we gotta learn this language. Cause how we gonna defend our rights if we speak one language an the police and teachers and politicians speak another?

Well, was one thing for my little kids to go to school, but was no way for me to go. I learn the language for the people I work with. Was only one problem. When it came to reading I was in big trouble. I had to depend on other people. How could I tell if the lawyer was not foolin me when we bought our house, or if the taxman was takin me for a fool?

As long as I had my kids around, understanding was not so hard. All the time I was thinkin of that old saying and find out that those sayings change when we come to this country. "Chi non va a scuola, non mai puo viaggiare solo." That's my new old saying that means, "Whoever doesn't go to school can never go anywhere alone."

So now I'm tryin to go to school. It's been three weeks since I started these night classes and already you can tell the difference in my words, eh? Let me tell you I still talk like I used to, but you can't tell so much in the writing, no?

It's a whole new world for me now that I can put down my own words. Oh, don't think old Pete is a genius student. My teacher correct all the mistakes I make and believea me they are so many. But I'm learning that in writing you can do things you can't do in speaking. You can hide in writing, like when a woman paints her face. You can take old wrinkles and make them disappear; you can make yourself more smart. You can do so many things.

But now I think back to that old saying and think maybe is true after all because when you read and when you write you have to stay by yourself. Is a hard thing for me to sit still when I read or write. I fine I always wann move my hands when I talk; how can you do that and write at the same time?

An another thing, you travel in your mind more when there's no one around and maybe that's what that old daying means. If you got to school, then you learn to travel alone. Chi sa? Well pretty soon I'm goan have my examination so I better study hard. Next time I tell you how I do.

TWENTY-THREE: APRIL 1987

I got some abad news for you. Old Pete has become a statistica. That's right. I'm joosta numero in the minus column. Iffa you doan know what that mean let me tell you simple. Moustache Pete is a dropout! That's right; a night school dropout. And to tell you the truth, I'mma happy man for it all.

I doan know what I was thinkin about when I try to go to school. I mean I have the right idea, you know; I'm old retire man with some time on his fingers and so I think maybe I could make up for some lost education. But instead of trust my first instincts, which tell me not to go to school but to learn some new things on my own, I went ahead to this evening school.

Now if you read last month then you know everything was goan pretty good. The teach she was helpin me with my mistakes when I write. And even I was getting to read a little bit better. Well then something happen that me me really craze. We was workin on reading and come my turn to read out loud.

We was reading from some workabook about how some poor boy come in America offa airplane and get lost. He could no speak English and alla time was askin for help. But no buddy unnerstan him. Now this poor by was talk to a police man when came my turn to read.

Well I wasa pretty nerves and was a little bit shaking in my hands. I start to read and the teach say, speak a little louder. So I raise up my voice and continue to read. Then the teach, she stop me again and say , "Please Mr. Baffo, stop putting letters in the words that aren't there."

And I say, "Well scusa me Miss Teach, but I doan know what you talkina bout." And she say, "Don't you hear yourself. Everytime you say a word, you but an "A" in between. Likea thisa. Anda that'sa not a righta."

I say, "Listen, is no my fault; I can no read the langueech chop, chop like my lips was scissors an my toungue wasa knife. I likea when the language she flow smooth. Besidesa I-a doan-a read-a the-a words-a like-a that-a. Sure every once in a while a few sounds get thrown in, but that's joosta the way I am.

And then she starts to get mad. She says," Well the least you can do is try. That's the way English is and if you don't even try, you shouldn't bother to come to these classes."

Well I tell her I promise to try, but no matter what, I fine I can no do it. So she sit me down.

Well I was sittin there and when class was over she come to me and say, "Listen, Mr. Baffo, you need to work on pronouncing. You can't sound the English language like that. And if I let you continue, then everyone is going to make fun of you.

I say, "Doan you worry for me. I'm use to it."

"Well then maybe this is not the right place for you," she says. "You tell me you've been coming here for all these weeks and you still can't tell that your still talking like you just got here."

Well that was too much for me and I blew up and say, "Listen, Miss Teach, you wasa not even born when I come here off the boat, so how do you know what I wasa soundin like way back then. Maybe I doan need this thing you call school All we do is sit in here and pronounce words I can't say and read things I don't care about.

"Now Mr. Baffo, that's not the right attitude for a beginning student," she says. "Well maybe is not so right for a begin student, but I think is pretty find for an end student."

"Go ahead, " she say. "Drop out and become a statistic. Join the other fifty percent of students who do the same. Instead of being a number that counts, you're going to be a number that's counted. And for all the wrong reasons."

Now I know she was talkin silly. What do numbers have to do with learning to read and write? So I say, "Did you ever ask youself why so many people drop out of you school?

"They drop out for many reasons," she say. "But most of those who do regret it."

"Wll this is one number statistica that doan regret nothin," I say, and then I walk out saying, "Thank you for your time, but for me was like I to walk inna store an forget what I come to buy."

So that's the story of my adult education. No maybe the reason an old dog can't learn new tricks, is because the old tricks still work. Besides, is getting to be warmer the weather, and I think I see a birdy on my back yard tree. And maybe, joosta maybe I'm goan back to Italy soon. Buona Pasqua a tutti quanti!

WORKS CITED

Barolini, Helen. "Introduction." *The Dream Book*. New York: Schocken, 1985. 3-56.

———. *Umbertina*. New York: Seaview. 1979.

Bassetti, Piero. *Italic Lessons*. New York: Bordighera P, 2010.

Covello, Leonard. *The Social Background of the Italo-American School Child*. Totowa, NJ: Rowman and Littlefield. 1972.

Fischer, Michael M. J. "Ethnicity and the Post-Modern Arts of Memory." *Writing Culture: The Poetics and Politics of Ethnography*. James Clifford and George E. Marcus, eds. Berkeley: U of California P, 1986. 194-233.

Gambino, Richard. "The Measure of Success." *Attenzione!* (July-August 1983): 14-15.

Gardaphe, Fred. *Moustache Pete is Dead*. New York: Bordighera Press, 1997.

Giovanni Agnelli Fondazione. *The Italian Americans: Who They Are, Where They Live, How Many They Are*. Torino: Fondazione G. Agnelli, 1980.

Greeley, Andrew. "Making it in America: Ethnic Groups and Social Status." *Social Policy* 4.2 (Sep/Oct 1973): 21-29.

McKenney, Nampeo R., Michael Levin and Alfred J. Tella. "A Sociodemographic Profile of Italian Americans." *Italian Americans: New Perspectives in Italian Immigration and Ethnicity*. Ed. Lydio Tomasi. New York: Center for Migration Studies of New York, Inc., 1985. 3-31.

Parinello, William. *Little Italy*. Documentary film, 1996.

Schwartz, Delmore. "In Dreams Begin Responsibilities." *In Dreams Begin Responsibilities and Other Stories*. New York: New Directions, 1938. 1-9.

Vecoli, Rudolph. "The Italian Americans: A New Generation is Rapidly Closing, the Gap Separating them from Others." *La Parola del Popolo*: 26.134 (September/October 1976): 45-53.

Yeats, William Butler. "Responsibilities." http://www.sacred-texts.com/neu/yeats/lpy/lpy080.htm.

Lessons from Once Dangerous Americans

MARIA LAURINO

Our country of immigrants has long been wary of its newest arrivals, with large swaths of citizens harboring an instinctual suspicion that "stranger always rhymes with danger" (Schiff 112), as the novelist Vladimir Nabokov once noted. The story of Italian Americans, who represented the largest group of immigrants coming to America during the great migration, not only provides historical lessons that can help unpack myths about today's immigrants, but also reveals the ethnic group's singular twentieth-century experience.

No other major American ethnic group had been at the center of *all* of the most tumultuous political events of twentieth century America—radical anarchism, nativism, Fascism, nationalism—as well as experiencing anti-religious fervor, racism, and association with organized crime. To have experienced such a staggering array of "isms" suggests that Italian Americans have a unique responsibility to speak out against the fear tactics and intimidation that many immigrants have experienced today under the administration of Donald Trump.

To understand the ability of Donald Trump, a man with no experience in elected office or government service, to become president of the United States, I want to begin by thinking of him as a modern-day epic storyteller, and here I'm borrowing the definition of an epic storyteller from the literary critic Robert Scholes. In *The Nature of Narrative* authors Robert Scholes and Robert Kellogg describe the epic storyteller as one whose primary impulse "is not a historical one, nor a creative one, it is re-creative. He is retelling a traditional story, and therefore his primary allegiance is not to fact, not to truth, not to entertainment, but to mythos itself. The word mythos meant precisely this in ancient Greece: a traditional story" (Scholes and Kellogg 12).

Donald Trump tells his epic tale—to Make America Great Again—in, albeit, a less Homeric than Homer Simpson-style of disconnected rambling speeches and tweets. Still, it is a traditional story that adheres not to history, not to fact, not to truth, but to mythos itself. His self-serving fables have imperiled American democracy, and democracy's survival may rest not just upon the checks and balances instituted by the founders, but upon our ability to make the past immediate, to use history as a means to resist and unmask falsehoods, and to serve as memory's guidepost. Let me begin with a story I call "A Tale of Two Shoemakers."

A little over one hundred years ago, two southern Italian men, like thousands of their impoverished brethren, arrived in the Boston area to work as shoemakers, settling in the then leather capital of the New World. Both were the same age—sixteen years old—when they came to Boston traveling among the hordes of impoverished peasants on passenger ships that left from the port of Naples. Each man would come to represent two myths about the immigrant experience. One would embody the nativist myth of the immigrant as dangerous stranger. The other would epitomize the belief that America's streets were paved with gold, a dream that lured millions to our shores.

One of our two shoemakers was trained in the art of handcrafting leather in Italy; the other learned here the piecemeal production line technique of edge trimming. Both responded similarly to the dehumanizing conditions of the early twentieth century factory: they were appalled, their spirits crushed.

Recording their impressions years later, one wrote: "This was not shoemaking, this was an inferno, a bedlam of rattles and clatters and whizzing machines and hurrying, scurrying people. I stood dazed" (Ferragamo 45).

The other explained to his young daughter: "the nightmare of the lower classes saddened very badly your father's soul" (Sacco 68).

Both eventually headed west, embarking on journeys that would forever alter their lives. One travelled to California and channeled his passion and disillusionment into making handcrafted shoes, paving the way for him to become a world-famous designer. The other went to Mexico and became radicalized living in close quarters with fellow anarchists who were plotting a world free of oppression and exploitation.

In 1927, the American journey would end for both men. That year, one of these two shoemakers, Salvatore Ferragamo, returned to Italy to perfect his dream, which he had successfully begun in America, of designing and making handcrafted shoes. The other shoemaker, Nicola Sacco, died in the electric chair along with Bartolomeo Vanzetti, the conclusion of a trial and seven-year legal process that revealed a shameful side of the American judicial system.

But this story is not just about two men and the synchronicity of their years here, as if each bookended a plot that twisted into tragedy for one, fame and fortune for the other. It is about what their lives represented to the wider world. And unfortunately for the Italian-American population, national leaders chose the narrative of Sacco and Vanzetti, not Ferragamo, to reaffirm their own ethnic prejudice and to spread the myth that Italians, incompatible with Anglo and Teutonic stock, were poisoning the American way of life.

To put this past into the context of today, one hundred years ago the prime candidates for the "next Boston bombers" — as Donald Trump called Muslim refugees marooned near Australia — would have been Italian Americans. That's because a small group of Italian-American anarchists, appalled by inhuman factory conditions and the use of child labor, believed in retaliatory violence, and were in fact making bombs in the Boston area that targeted capitalists and government officials who had suppressed strikes and other radical activity.

In the early twentieth century, anarchism was the terrorist threat on American soil. After a Polish anarchist assassinated President William McKinley, the government outlawed anarchism in America, but still it took root. Nicola Sacco and Bartolomeo Vanzetti were convicted of murder in the payroll robbery of a shoe factory. The government had little evidence against Sacco and Vanzetti for this crime, but they were targeted, perhaps framed, by the police because of their radical activity. Both men were followers of a small but violent and messianic anarchist movement led by an Italian named Luigi Galleani.

They were faithful members of Galleani's Gruppo Autonomo, a Boston-based anarchist group planning a world without government that could match their utopian dreams. Galleani, a fiery and mesmerizing leader, preached that by eliminating laws, private property, and the profit motive, men and women could lead fulfilling, ethical lives without the constrictions of church or state. The anarchists provided community for immigrants, offering spirited lectures and picnics and theater groups, in which they acted out these utopian ideas. But Galleani's group also advocated violence to achieve their lofty goals.

Of course, the vast majority of Italian immigrants had no connection to radical anarchism. Underpaid, overworked, and trying to establish a new life in America, they were paving the streets and producing the garments and goods this newly industrialized country needed and craved. Many were injured, some were killed on the job, like my maternal great-grandfather, and, still, they earned so little money that their families went hungry.

I'd like to suggest that this tale of two shoemakers might help us interpret the stories, and the myths, that shape our perception of the world. It could help us think about how we act, and how we will react to the plight of today's immigrants who face many of the same issues that once plagued Italian Americans. Ferragamo's horror of factory life was primarily aesthetic—he was appalled that people worked in terrible conditions to make an inferior product. "Heavy, clumsy, and brutal," he wrote of mass production, "not to be compared even with the shoes I had seen in Naples. I stared and wandered miserably. How could I choose a job in this labyrinth?" (Ferragamo 45).

Sacco's response, on the other hand, was not aesthetic but ethical. He was never a craftsman like Ferragamo, believing above all else in his ability to make something beautiful with his hands; he was a highly skilled piecemeal worker who earned an excellent living—considered by one of his employers the best of over three thousand edge trimmers he had hired—and happily married with a child.

He was also deeply compassionate and read about other workers, who saw no other recourse but to go on strike, be brutally suppressed by factory owners. These inhumane conditions turned Sacco into an anarchist. But—and this is a significant qualifier—as a follower of Galleani, Sacco became so convinced of the rightness of his point of view that he accepted the idea of armed revolution to overthrow the existing order.

Galleani sought what he called "the Ideal"—a world free of government, law, property, and religion. He published a 46-page bomb manual called *La salute è in voi!* (Health is in you!") as a training guide for radicals. As history reminds us, violent extremism and utopian visions take both secular and religious forms.

The work of Princeton scholar Paul Avrich, who published in 1991 *Sacco and Vanzetti: The Anarchist Background*, put the beliefs of Sacco and Vanzetti in a new historical light. Sacco and Vanzetti's trial was heavily biased against them—the trial judge and other authorities were rigidly set against these men who were foreigners, atheists, and anarchists. A fair trial was impossible in such a setting, and the prosecution techniques, coaching witnesses and perhaps even tampering with the physical evidence, revealed a dark time for the American judicial system.

Sacco and Vanzetti, however, were not pacifists or naïfs, as many have portrayed them. The ethical ideas and whimsical musings conveyed in the hundreds of letters they wrote in prison contradict the affiliations and friendships they both kept with violent bombers, or perhaps reveal the darkest contradictions and rationalizations of the human soul.

The *Galleanisti*, dangerous and violent as they were, did have a bit of a gang-that-couldn't-shoot-straight quality to them. In 1916, a Galleani follower tried to assassinate the new Roman Catholic cardinal of Chicago at a banquet honoring him by putting arsenic in the soup. But the anarchist chef, a little too heavy-handed with the arsenic, poured so much into the steaming pot that the two hundred guests in the room merely vomited it up.

In 1919, Galleani's group mailed letter bombs in thirty packages to capitalists, jurists, and political figures who suppressed strikes and radical action, including John D. Rockefeller, J.P. Morgan, and

Oliver Wendell Holmes. Although the bombs were sophisticated devices, the anarchists naively thought these men opened their own mail, making their first victim a southern black maid who lost her hand opening the package.

But even worse for their plan, over half of the boxes languished in the post office because of insufficient postage. The anarchists' scheme and dream—to have all the bombs explode on May Day—failed because someone neglected to lick enough stamps. They regrouped the next month and decided to blow up the house of U.S. Attorney General A. Mitchell Palmer, who lived across the street from Franklin Roosevelt. But echoing the macabre slapstick of "insufficient postage" and arsenic-laced soup, the assailant either tripped or improperly timed the fuse, and the bomb blew him up.

The dead man was later identified as the Italian anarchist Carlo Valdinoci, a friend of Sacco and Vanzetti's, and Valdinoci's sister came to live with the Saccos after her brother's death. Another friend of Sacco and Vanzetti's, Mario Buda, was tied to several Gruppo Autonomo bombings and is believed responsible for the Wall Street explosions set off five days after the indictment of Sacco and Vanzetti—most likely in protest—that killed thirty-three people and wounded over two hundred, causing America's greatest terrorist disaster of the time.

They were, in the lingo of Donald Trump, some "bad hombres"—or more specifically ultra militant *paesani*—but they represented the tiniest subset of a large, hard-working ethnic group.

Here is probably a good point to return to our other story, that of the Italian-American cobbler who at sixteen left his impoverished village of Bonito in the province of Avellino with only a third grade education and rigorous training in handcrafting leather.

It took merely one day at the Queen Quality Shoe Manufacturing Company in Boston for Ferragamo to pack his bags. He decided that, despite how bad life in southern Italy had been, he would need to find work outside of this demoralizing New England factory system. It was 1914, and within a week he left, headed west to California on a train car to join his siblings settled in Santa Barbara, who mailed him a life-saving ticket for the cross-country journey.

One brother, who had also abandoned the same Boston shoe factory because of an aggravated shoulder injury, became a tailor for the American Film Company. This brother suggested that the nascent studio might need a shoemaker's skills.

The idea proved ingenious and soon Salvatore, attending school at night to learn English, was carving leather for cowboy boots for the actor Douglas Fairbanks and fitting delicate pumps for Lottie Pickford.

In the 1920s, Ferragamo moved to Los Angeles, where he received his largest commission and first major breakthrough, designing the shoe wardrobe for Cecil B. DeMille's mammoth 1923 production, *The Ten Commandments.* Moses led his people to the promised land wearing Egyptian-style sandals designed by Ferragamo.

America's expansive education system enabled Ferragamo to enroll as an evening student at the University of Southern California. A course in human anatomy helped him understand how to make stylish shoes more comfortable by aligning the design with the natural balance of the standing body, which Ferragamo determined dropped "vertically on the arches of the feet." Correspondence courses, founded to allow immigrants to be educated for specific professions, allowed Ferragamo to continue his studies in chemical engineering and mathematics. He was seeking new ways to treat leather and develop applications for different materials.

Sacco also headed west, to Mexico in 1917 with fellow Galleani followers to avoid the draft for World War I and to plan a return to Italy. That was the year in which the Russian czar had been toppled and the Galleanisti believed that a world revolution was soon to come — and they wanted to fight in Europe for those ideals.

The U.S. government was now tightly cracking down on radical and unpatriotic activity, sentencing, for example, Eugene Debs to ten years in prison merely for making an antiwar speech. This zealous suppression of free speech began a vicious cycle of government repression and radical response, and the anarchists became more and more convinced that violent action had to be taken.

When it became clear that the revolution wasn't spreading across Europe, the anarchists—and Sacco and Vanzetti met in Mexico the most militant of Galleani's followers—decided to concentrate their resources in America. By 1919, acts of violence across the country took place. After the attempted bombing of the house of the Attorney General the government frantically sought the perpetrators. When they discovered an anarchist's leaflet near the explosion and traced it to the Gruppo Autonomo, the government began to close in on Galleani's group.

It was under these circumstances that police arrested Sacco and Vanzetti for the robbery in South Braintree, Massachusetts in 1920 with little credible evidence against them. Two men had been murdered in a payroll robbery of a shoe factory, and a police chief decided that anarchists trying to finance their activities, not a previously suspected gang of local thugs, had committed the crime. The evidence against both men was so weak that it exposed the prejudices and limitations of the American judicial system and created a worldwide outrage over the men's executions.

During a lengthy appeals process, mounting evidence pointed to this local gang who specialized in stealing shipments from shoe manufacturers, not Sacco and Vanzetti, yet neither the Governor of Massachusetts nor the President of Harvard, who headed an advisory committee about the case, would recommend a new trial.

Instead, despite worldwide outrage about the lack of a fair trial, the execution was carried out and the Sacco and Vanzetti case became a symbol of the government's overarching narrative of southern Italians as dangerous anarchists, socialists, and mafia members.

Thematically, a shoe factory again figures into our story—this time as motivation for robbery and murder—the image of shoes resurfacing in each man's life as a nightmare or a dream. To try to unpack how myths are translated into the cultural landscape, let me borrow from Western culture's most famous interpreters of dreams and symbols, Freud and Jung. Both men, as British historian and mythographer Marina Warner writes, analyzed "narratives, learned and popular, in order to unlock symbolic, psychic explanations of human consciousness and behaviour" (Warner 19).

Applying this kind of symbolic reading to the nativist myth of Italian Americans as inherently untrustworthy—with Sacco and Vanzetti's radical activity representing that of the broader Italian community—metaphorically, the sole of shoemaker Sacco's product was crushing the soul of the nation's tolerance. But if we had simply turned our heads to the west coast, choosing instead the model of the Ferragamo story to represent the Italian immigrant experience, the sole of the shoemaker's creation was lifting America's desires. The overarching myth of desirable Americans versus undesirable immigrants reveals a troubling repetition in the patterns of human behavior. One hundred years later, the target of our anger and fear gets replaced by a new, seemingly threatening group.

A popular cartoon at the beginning of the twentieth century, depicting the United States as the "Unrestricted Dumping Ground" bringing rats "direct from the slums of Europe daily," succinctly illustrates nativist prejudice—the same prejudices that would play into the Sacco and Vanzetti trial. Lined up are the dark rats of anarchism, socialism, and the Mafia ready to commit murder and poison Uncle Sam's pure America. Replace this cartoon's words with "radical Islamic terrorism" and "direct from the slums of the Muslim world daily" and we have today's traditional nativist tale told by our mythic storyteller president who took office seeking to impose a Muslim ban.

THE UNRESTRICTED DUMPING-GROUND.

Judge Magazine, June 6, 1903

As we have witnessed in America, Europe, and around the world, this populist tale is spreading. An editor from the local newspaper of the rural Australian town where an ISIS suspect was arrested in March, 2017 wrote: "One argument developing is that Muslims cannot be trusted, they are all bad, and with so many in our town, it was only a matter of time before trouble raised its head. The other point put forward is that hatred is not the way to handle this situation and one man's actions should not condemn the entire town's Muslim population."

In addressing these two present-day scenarios, history can serve as our guidepost. To look today, without the thick layers of Anglo-Saxon prejudice, at the over seventeen million descendants of those early Italian immigrants, the overwhelming story of this population has been one of loyalty, pride, dedication, fortitude, and relentless hard work.

Salvatore Ferragamo's determination to escape his impoverished past to pursue his personal dream, one in which ingenuity and determination could propel a cobbler who once pounded leather in a tiny stone room in southern Italy to establish a global luxury brand, reflects the American ideal of possibility and renewal. The majority of immigrants would not achieve Ferragamo's international success and fame. But success was achieved in escaping a land without hope to make a new life here. Still, it would take at least another half-century to create the tolerance to fully appreciate this version of the Italian-American immigrant story in the larger American society.

As the Trump administration's attempt at a Muslim ban was a crude overreaction to today's radical threat, the Sacco and Vanzetti trial spurred a nativist reaction and movement that led to the most restrictive immigration act in America. A key expert witness to the Congressional immigration committee testified that the American stock had been polluted by "alien hereditary degeneracy"—a phrase that sounds an awful lot like today's Twitter feed of Congressman Steve King. The Johnson-Reed Act of 1924 created a strict quota system, drastically cutting the number of people who could emigrate from Southern and Eastern Europe.

By the end of the 1920s, this small anarchist movement was severely on the wane. Anarchists who worked with the budding labor movement and didn't support violence, like Carlo Tresca, would become leaders of an important group of anti-Fascists in the 1930s, courageously standing up to the majority here who supported Mussolini's right-wing dictatorship. And even among the small anarchist population, most never resorted to, or believed in violence. The Italian immigrant sculptor Ugo Lavaggi, who worked for the renowned studio of the Piccirilli Brothers, was an atheist, probably an anarchist, yet he carved out of marble from Carrara, Italy one of the greatest contributions to American political art—the head of Abraham Lincoln on the Lincoln Memorial.

This tale of two shoemakers is a reminder that our nation of immigrants has always been wary of its newest arrivals. If those in charge have a nativist outlook, they place a disproportionate emphasis on outliers, tarring entire communities for the misdeeds of the few, and stirring frenzy among the populace about the danger of strangers.

❧

Marina Warner describes a myth as "a kind of story told in public, which people tell one another; they wear an air of ancient wisdom, but that is part of their seductive charm.... [M]yth's own secret cunning means that it pretends to present the matter as it is and always must be, at its heart lies the principle, in the famous formula of Roland Barthes, that history is turned into nature."

"But, contrary to this understanding," Warner continues, "myths aren't writ in stone, they're not fixed, but often … change dramatically both in content and meaning. Myths offer a lens which can be used to see human identity in its social and cultural context—they can lock us up in stock reactions, bigotry and fear, but they're not immutable, and by unpicking them, the stories can lead to others" (19).

To unpick some of these myths, as Warner suggests, allows old stories to lead to new ones. That's why it's important for Italian Americans to recognize in Trump's central campaign myth another disturbing echo from earlier in the twentieth century. Italian Americans are in the unique position of having been front and center of the most tumultuous political events of the twentieth century. This experience, of not only being the victims of discrimination and suspicion, but also of having our patriotism and loyalty questioned and doubted, calls upon us to remain vigilant in preventing twentieth-century authoritarian political movements from rising again in new forms.

Putting aside for a moment both the racist and anti-immigrant connotations of Make America Great Again, this myth calls to mind an Italian one—that only one leader could return Italy to the glory of its past, to "the fateful destiny of Rome."

In other words, only one man, the dictator Benito Mussolini, could Make Italy Great Again. When this myth was finally punctured, Italy's cities had been bombed, its economy devastated, and the country's moral stature, having aligned with Hitler's Germany, eroded.

But a decade earlier, Italians, Italian Americans, and many prominent Americans fervently believed the myth of Mussolini. As historian and anthropologist David I. Kertzer wrote: "What he understood, in a way none of his predecessors had, was that people were ruled most of all by emotion, and that their reality had less to do with the external world than with the symbolic one he could fashion for them" (62).

This quote could just as easily apply to Donald Trump, who, in essence, has said the same thing about himself: "I play to people's fantasies." During the presidential campaign Trump even tweeted a quote attributed to Mussolini: "Better to live one day as a lion than 100 years as sheep."

Donald Trump has been compared to Benito Mussolini; he's also been compared to Silvio Berlusconi. Trump's admiration for authoritarian leaders and his totalitarian instincts are what draw comparisons to dictators and autocrats around the world, including Vladimir Putin and Recep Tayyip Erdogan in Turkey. For what are "alternative facts" but the imaginary underpinnings of a symbolic world that match a man's psychological needs or fulfill a people's emotional desires.

Government released photographs that show sparse Inauguration Day crowds compared to the numbers who came to see Barack Obama should serve as an objective record of that January day, but Donald Trump spoke of huge crowds — huger than ever before — to fit his epic tale, the mythic adulatory beginning of his presidency. He then sent out his press secretary to demand that America's free press report it was "the largest audience to witness an inauguration, period," a now infamous, parodied line, but one that could have come from the playbook of Mussolini.

There is another trait that both men share — the embrace of contradiction. Mussolini, an atheist and socialist, began his career as a journalist supporting striking factory workers in Lawrence, Massachusetts, joining the same cause as Nicola Sacco. Yet, once in power, he courted the head of J.P. Morgan bank and forged a groundbreaking alliance with the Pope and Catholic Church. The once-atheist dictator put crucifixes in every classroom to win the

Catholic Church's approval, and the signing of the Lateran Accords with Pope Pius XI ended the separation of Church of State in Italy that had been in place since the birth of the Italian Republic. Mussolini, like Trump, continually contradicted his earlier beliefs because his primary allegiance was always and only to himself.

It's important to remember that from the early 1920s to the mid-1930s, our country believed the Mussolini myth. Government leaders, prominent Americans, and the mainstream media considered Mussolini the only man who could stop the tide of Bolshevism from spreading into Europe. There was also a good amount of anti-Italian bias in America's ardor for the dictator. While the country's elite detested southern Italian immigrants, they admired the north of Italy for its great beauty, art, and architecture. But a country fueled by a Protestant work ethic held little space for art, beauty, and leisure, and Americans considered Italians inefficient and unproductive. Italy may be a beautiful country, this type of thinking went, but someone needed to make the trains run on time. And America believed that someone was Mussolini.

The humorist Will Rogers, in a sycophantic interview in Mussolini's office, laughed with the dictator about his practice of force-feeding pints of castor oil to those who opposed him. The point of castor oil was to make the victim soil himself in front of the Fascist thugs and then suffer days of unbearable stomach cramps.

During Will Roger's years-long "bromance" with the dictator, he wrote that Mussolini "has done more things for his country … than any hundred men in any other country," that Mussolini could run America "with his eyes shut," and that "Dictator form of government is the greatest form of government there is, if you have the right Dictator."

The humorist James Thurber was so upset by Will Roger's support for Mussolini that two decades later he wrote about Roger's "irresponsible behavior," which revealed how "political satire can be as dangerous as an unguided missile when it is unsound." Such widespread admiration among America's native sons made it easy for many Italian Americans to embrace Mussolini; it allowed them to escape the strict confines of being typecast as stolid laborers or labor agitators and anarchists. Here was a man who could lessen their humiliation, illustrate their devotion to religion and country, and restore pride and glory to the Italy of their imagination. Nothing helps the confidence of a marginalized and maligned ethnic group more than recognizing that a new American idol is one of your own.

But by the 1940s, Italian Americans paid deeply for their enthusiasm. Some of President Roosevelt's generals were convinced that a fifth column existed in this country taking its orders from Roberto, that is, Rome, Berlin, Tokyo, and they targeted Italian Americans. Two days after the attack on Pearl Harbor, Italian nationals—many of them our grandmothers who never bothered to take the citizenship test—were labeled "enemy aliens," their movements monitored and restricted, and they were forced to carry a pink identification card at all times. Over ten thousand Italians who lived on the west coast deemed enemy aliens were forcibly removed from their homes, again many were old women, with the government treating grandmas as if they were sautéing bombs for the gravy or packing pistols in Sunday purses, alongside the rosary beads.

When we approached the new millennium, many believed that the evils particular to the twentieth century would be left behind. We had new problems, new threats, but figures like Benito Mussolini, jutting his jaw, preening, seemed a comic figure relegated to history. Political analysts like George Bush's former speechwriter David Frum are warning today of what Umberto Eco, the brilliant Italian novelist, critic, and professor of semiotics cautioned several decades ago—that if Fascism arises again it will not appear in the same guise as the old. It won't be found in scenes like the hordes of people cheering and chanting for Mussolini on the balcony of Rome's Piazza Venezia. Rather, the crowds would be replaced, Eco warned, by an "*'Internet populism,'* in which the emotional response of a selected group of citizens can be presented and accepted as the 'voice of the people.'"

Eco's prescient lecture given at Columbia University in 1995 detailed the characteristics of what he called "Ur-Fascism," or Eternal Fascism. He argued that Fascism has always been harder to define than, say, Nazism, because "Mussolini had no philosophy: all he had was rhetoric." But that if you examine the regime's way of thinking and feeling, its cultural habits, you can begin to see the patterns of what composed Mussolini's state.

The patterns and characteristics Eco cited include:

- a cult of traditionalism in which there can be no advancement of learning because the truth is already known;
- a cult of action for action's sake;
- the belief that dissent amounts to betrayal;
- a movement that springs from individual and social frustration;
- a staunch nationalism that appeals to those with no social identity and tells them that the only privilege is the supremacy of the native born.

Machismo and contempt for women are also signs of Ur-Fascism as the leader "transfers his will to power onto sexual questions.... Since sex is also a difficult game to play, the Ur-Fascist hero plays with weapons." Eco concluded his list with the trait of Newspeak from George Orwell's *1984*. The aim of Newspeak, he explains, is "to limit the instruments available to complex and critical reasoning" (78-86).

Twitter becomes the perfect conduit for this Ur-Fascist trait, allowing societal and world complexities to be reduced to: BAD, SAD, FAKE, and HOAX. Umberto Eco pleaded for every citizen dedicated to individual freedom to look for the traits of Ur-Fascism, to unmask them, and to "point the finger at each of its new forms—every day, in every part of the world." His words remind us that our freedom is never guaranteed.

History has taught us how intolerant judges and political figures, convinced of the incompatibility of Italians to fit in with American stock, would convict immigrants of crimes based on flimsy, perhaps even fixed evidence.

History has taught us how government overreaction resulted in our parents, grandparents, or great-grandparents being forced to carry enemy alien identification cards and be forcibly removed from their homes;

History has taught that years of hard manual labor and loyalty to America could be rendered meaningless if the population chooses to believe those who repeat myths as if they were ancient oracles writ in stone, rather than stories that people tell one another, stories that we have the power to change.

Myth and fantasy play powerful roles in how people see themselves and act in the world. Italian Americans can help to puncture prevailing myths by learning and sharing our history. By coming together as an assembly of citizens who recognize that our roots were once planted in inhospitable American soil, that it would take decades, nearly a century, of untwisting these gnarled branches before new generations could thrive without stumbling, without being condescended to, without explaining or apologizing, without having to undo pieces of ourselves by lopping off vowels on our names, or pretending we're from Florence instead of from the land, as peasants once described, where even Christ forgot to stop—all in the hope of escaping those ugly and crude caricatures assigned to Italian Americans by the majority culture.

This knowledge should allow us to call upon the lessons of our past as a means of uniting in a common history and humanity, of showing empathy for people, who like us, were never dangerous strangers, but desperate, endangered, and impoverished, leaving behind what they knew and loved for this promise that we have always called America.

References

Paul Avrich, *Sacco and Vanzetti: The Anarchist Background*, Princeton, NJ: Princeton University Press.

Peter Carlson, *American History Magazine*, "Encounter: Will Rogers Befriends Benito Mussolini," November 8, 2016.

Umberto Eco, "Ur-Fascism," from *Five Moral Pieces*, New York: Harcourt, 2002.

Salvatore Ferragamo, *Shoemaker of Dreams: The Autobiography of Salvatore Ferragamo*, Florence: Centro Di, 1985, p. 45.

David I. Kertzer, *The Pope and Mussolini: The Secret History of Pius XI and the Rise of Fascism in Europe*, New York, Random House, 2014.

New York Times, "Arrest of ISIS Suspect in Rural Town Puts Australia on Edge," March 9, 2017

Nicola Sacco, Bartolomeo Vanzetti, *The Letters of Sacco and Vanzetti*, New York: Penguin, 2007.

Stacy Schiff, *Véra (Mrs. Vladimir Nabokov)*, New York: Random House, 1999.

Robert E. Scholes and Robert Kellogg, *The Nature of Narrative*, Oxford: Oxford University Press, 1968.

John Schwartz, *New York Times Book Review*, "Will Rogers, Populist Cowboy," March 25, 2011.

Marina Warner, "Monstrous Mothers," from *Six Myths of Our Time*, New York: Random House, 1995.

Bruce Watson, *Sacco and Vanzetti: The Men, the Murders, and the Judgment of Mankind*, New York: Viking, 2007.

Virtual Sambuca
Research in Rural Sicily Before and After the Digital Revolution

Donna R. Gabaccia

Google the term "Sambuca," and today's WorldWideWeb generously delivers 4.86 million "hits" for the eager researcher's further exploration. Most of the pages identified by the Google Search Engine discuss the liqueur Sambuca Romana (Sambuca Molinari), manufactured since World War II in Civitavecchia, in central Italy. The popularity of this drink explains why so many of my English-speaking Canadian, American or Italian-American friends tell me they "love Sambuca," when they learn I did my earliest research in a town of that name. I've never tasted Sambuca and my research site was in Sicily.[1] Obviously, there have long been several Sambucas in Italy and in today's world, knowledge of Sambuca emerges from the digital realm. This paper explores the possibility that the digital revolution of the past thirty years has also changed the ways scholars like me understand Sambuca, a town of just under 6000 residents located in the south western Sicilian province of Agrigento.

Even before the digital revolution scholars knew a great deal about Sambuca di Sicilia (until 1928 named Sambuca Zabut). In the nineteenth century, this Sambuca was home to 10,000 peasants, artisans and local gentry. It was a typical Sicilian "agrotown" which means it was no village but a surprisingly dense urban settlement. Historically, Sambuca's urbanity forced thousands of its peasant residents to walk long distances to the fields where they cultivated wheat for sale and raised their own food.[2] After a 1968 earthquake, Sambuca gradually acquired a suburb of attractive,

---

[1] There is also Sambuca Pistoiese, in Toscana. In my Toronto neighborhood there are two different cafés bearing the name Sambuca, most likely honoring the liqueur rather than any Italian town.

[2] Jane and Peter Schneider, *Culture and Political Economy in Western Sicily* (New York: Academic Press, 1976); Donna Gabaccia, *From Sicily to Elizabeth Street: Housing and Social Change among Italian Immigrants, 1880-1930* (Albany: SUNY Press, 1984).

new homes *fuori paese*.³ Today, the town center remains occupied, but has become less desirable as a residential location causing locals to worry about depopulation.⁴ The number of residents has in fact fallen by almost half over the past century, in part as a result of emigration to North and South America, northern Europe and northern Italy and in part because Sambucesi sharply reduced the size of their families.⁵ Sambuca differs from other Sicilian towns in one important respect; after 1945, it consistently elected Communists to municipal offices.⁶ At the time I began research there, Sambucesi were both proud of their *roccaforte rossa* ("red citadel") and worried younger generations were losing interest in politics.

Beginning a half century ago, an eclectic, interdisciplinary group of scholars began to study Sambuca as both representative of and unique among Sicily's agrotowns. In 1958, local intellectuals founded Sambuca's newspaper, *La Voce di Sambuca*, which understood its mandate to interpret the past as well as the present. Anthropologists Jane and Peter Schneider arrived in Sambuca in the mid-1960s and I, an historian, first visited in 1977. Between 1976 and 1998, we three American scholars wrote four books and two dozen articles about Sambuca.⁷ (In the publications authored by Jane and Peter

---

³ Called by locals *la zona di trasferimento*, it now has its own church, San Giorgio, with its own festival day on April 23; its street names, meanwhile, read like a small catalog of local, national and international leftist activists, including martyrs across the political spectrum and including both Aldo Moro and Sacco and Vanzetti. For interpretations of Sambuca' history of leftist activism, see n. 6.

⁴ See "Sambuca incentive il turismo: Case in vendita a 1 Euro," *Belice News*, April 15, 2018. https://belicenews.it/turismo/sambuca-di-sicilia/sambuca-incentiva-il-turismo-case-in-vendita-a-1-euro/?utm_source=dlvr.it&utm_medium=facebook. Accessed April 28, 2018.

⁵ Jane and Peter Schneider, *Festival of the Poor: Fertility Decline and the Ideology of Class in Sicily, 1860-1930* (Tucson: University of Arizona Press, 1996).

⁶ Donna Gabaccia, *Militants and Migrants: Rural Sicilians become American Workers* (New Brunswick: Rutgers University Press, 1988); see also Salvatore Maurici, *Lotte contadine e movimenti democratici* (Sambuca: La Voce di Sambuca, 1992) and Salvatore Maurici, *Testimonianze e breve storia del PCI a Sambuca di Sicilia* (Sambuca: Circolo di Rifondazione comunista, 2000).

⁷ The books are cited in n. 2, 5 and 6. Articles based on Sambuca research by Gabaccia include "Neither Padrone Slaves nor Primitive Rebels," in Dirk Hoerder, ed., *Struggle a Hard Battle, Essays on Immigrant Radicals* (DeKalb: Northern

Illinois University Press, 1986); "Kinship, Culture and Migration: A Sicilian Example," *Journal of American Ethnic History* (Spring 1984): 39-53; "Migration and Peasant Militance, Western Sicily, 1880-1910," *Social Science History* (Winter 1984): 67-80; "Sicilians in Space: Environmental Change and Family Geography," *Journal of Social History* (Winter 1982): 53-66; "Housing and Household Work, Sicily and New York, 1890-1910," *Michigan Occasional Papers in Women's Studies* (1981). Articles by Peter Schneider include "Honor and Conflict in a Sicilian Town," *Anthropological Quarterly* 42 (1969): 130-155; "Coalition Formation and Colonialism in Western Sicily," *European Journal of Sociology* 13 (1972): 255-267; "Rural Artisans and Peasant Mobilization in the Socialist International: the *Fasci Siciliani*," *The Journal of Peasant Studies* 13 (1986): 63-81. Articles by Jane Schneider include "Family Patrimonies and Economic Behavior in Western Sicily," *Anthropological Quarterly* 42 (1969): 109-130; "Of Vigilance and Virgins: Honor, Shame, and Access to Resources in the Mediterranean," *Ethnology* 10 (1971): 1-25; "Trousseau as Treasure: Some Contradictions of Late Nineteenth Century Change in Sicily," in Eric Ross, ed., *Behind the Myth of Culture* (New York: Academic Press, 1980). Articles co-authored by Jane and Peter Schneider include "Urbanization in Sicily: two contrasting models," in L.A. La Ruffa, et al, eds., City and Peasant: a Study in Sociocultural Dynamics, *Annals of the New York Academy of Science*, Vol. 220 (1974): 496-508; "Peasants Speak: Sicilian Harvest Song," *Journal of Peasant Studies* (1974): 390-95; "Economic dependency and the failure of cooperatives in western Sicily," in N.S. Hopkins, et al, eds., *Popular Participation in Social Change: Cooperatives and Nationalized Industry* (Amsterdam: Mouton, 1976); "The Reproduction of the ruling class in Sicily, 1850-1920," in George Marcus, ed., *The Anthropological Study of Elites* (Albuquerque, New Mexico: University of New Mexico Press, 1983); "The dissolution of ruling elites in twentieth century Sicily," in George Marcus, ed., *The Anthropological Study of Elites* (Albuquerque, New Mexico: University of New Mexico Press, 1983); "Demographic transitions in a Sicilian rural town," *The Journal of Family History*, Special Issue on History and Anthropology, 9 (1984): 245-273; "Sex and Respectability in an Age of Fertility Decline: A Sicilian Case Study," *Social Science and Medicine* 33,8 (1981): 885-895; "Going Forward in Reverse Gear: Culture, Economy and Political Economy in the Demographic Transitions of a Sicilian Rural Town," in Gillis, John R., Louise A. Tilly, and David Levine, (eds.) *The European Experience of Declining Fertility, 1850-1970: A Quiet Revolution* (Cambridge MA & Oxford UK: Blackwell, 1992), pp. 146-174; "High Fertility and Poverty in Sicily: Beyond the Culture vs. Rationality Debate," pp. 179-202 in Susan Greenhalgh (ed.) *Situating Fertility; Anthropology and Demographic Inquiry* (Cambridge University Press, 1995); "Coitus Interruptus and Family Respectability in Catholic Europe: A Sicilian Case Study," pp. 177-195 in Rapp, Rayna and Faye Ginsburg (eds.) *Conceiving the New World Order; Global Politics of Reproduction* (Los Angeles: University of California Press, 1995); "Political Economy and Cultural Processes in the Fertility Decline of Sicilian Artisans", pp. 177-197 in Alaka Malwade Basu and Peter Aaby (eds.) *The Methods and Uses of Anthropological Demography* (Oxford: Oxford University Press, Clarendon Press, 1998).

Schneider, Sambuca appeared as Villamaura, a pseudonym borrowed from a novel written in the nineteenth century by local intellectual Emanuele Navarro della Miraglia.[8]) Their books and articles analyzed domestic life and material culture, political economy, labor militancy, the fertility transition, and transnational migration out of and returning to the town. After 1980, Sambuca's local intellectuals hastened the pace of scholarly production. Writing in dialect and in Italian, they made scholarship on the town's political and intellectual history and its folklore accessible to Sambuca's residents.[9]

---

[8] Emanuele Navarro della Miraglia, *La Nana* (Milano: Brigola, 1879). Sambuca's municipal library is named after Emanuele Navarro della Miraglia's father. For a brief biography (that explains his choice of "della Miraglia" as a nom de plume, see Francesco Lucioli, "Navarro della Miraglia, Emanuele," *Dizionario Biografico degli Italiani*, vol. 78: http://www.treccani.it/enciclopedia/navarro-della-miraglia-emanuele_(Dizionario-Biografico)/ Accessed online April 29, 2018.

[9] In addition to books cited in n. 6, see *Sambuca di Sicilia e la Madonna dell'Udienza: 80. Anniversario dell' incoronazione, 1903-1983* (Sambuca: Pro Loco Adragna Carboj, Confraternità Maria SS. Dell'Udienza, 1983); Alfonso Di Giovanna, *Alla scoperta della terra di Zabut* (Sambuca di Sicilia : pro-loco Adragna Carboj, 1985); Salvatore Maurici, *Briganti sambucesi* (Palermo: Lo studente, 1985); Salvatore Maurici, *Chabuca: Cunti e canti* (Palermo: Lo studente, 1985); Baldassare Gurrera, *Idilliche visioni* (Sambuca di Sicilia: Biblioteca comunale, 1987); Amedeo Pepe, et al., ed., *Sicilia: così il Natale...: poesie, detti, proverbi, canti popolari, indovinelli, scongiuri* (Sambuca di Sicilia: Centro civiltà mediterranea, 1989); Salvatore Maurici, *Andrea Maurici (1857-1936): critico, storico, letterato* (Sambuca di Sicilia: Centro civiltà mediterranea, 1991); *Conference Proceedings, 1902-1992, 90 anni del Circolo Operai Girolamo Guasto, una realtà significatica a Sambuca* (Palermo: Genio, 1993); Agostino Mangiaracina, ed., *Fra Felice da Sambuca* (Sciacca: Rotary club, 1995); Anna Lo Jacono, *Poesie* (Sambuca di Sicilia: Biblioteca Comunale "V. Navarro," 1996); Alfonso Di Giovanna, *Per modo di dire: storie e leggende della Terra di Zabut* (Sambuca di Sicilia: La voce editrice-Zabut, 1997); Maria Concetta Di Natale, ed., *Segni mariani nella terra dell'emiro: la Madonna dell'Udienza a Sambuca di Sicilia tra devozione e arte* (Sambuca: Banca di credito cooperativo, 1997); Salvatore Maurici, *Ingiurii a la Sammuca: sopranomi a Sambuca di Sicilia* (Salemi: Centro studi solidale, 1998); Gaetano Bongiovanni, *Antonio Guarino: pittore e incisore del primo novecento* (Sambuca di Sicilia: Banca di credito cooperativo di Sambuca, 2000); Alfonso Di Giovanna, *Ilaria d'Inghilterra* (Sambuca di Sicilia: Istituzione Giambecchina, 2000) Giusy Marino, *Lu me paasatempu: poesia in lingua siciliana* (Sambuca: Grafiche "La Risorgente," 2000); *5. Rassegna d'arte: pittori e poeti sambucesi*, (Sambuca di Sicilia, [s. n.], 2005); Giuseppe Cacioppo, *Vulgo Audienzia appellata: la devozione alla Madonna dell'Udienza a Sambuca di Sicilia nella cultura figurativa siciliana* (S. l.: s. n., 2008); Salvatore Maurici, *Stazzuna e stazzunara: economia e tradizione a Sambuca di Sicilia* (Sambuca di Sicilia: Polilabor, 2012).

This sizeable scholarly corpus was largely completed by the time the digital revolution reached Sambuca at the turn of the millenium. Sambuca thus offers an ideal site from which to ponder the impact of the digital revolution on scholarship, for the older research creates a baseline for comparison to newer, digital forms of knowledge. Because the digital revolution has transformed so many aspects of everyday life--think of social media, email, the worldwide web, Google, Amazon, streaming forms of digital entertainment and games, and the ubiquity of smart phone and Skype communication—readers may imagine comparably dramatic revolutions occurring in scholarship. Certainly, statements about the revolutionary potential of digital tools, methods, and data for the transformation of scholarship are easily found.[10] Yet no studies I know have documented cases of scholarship being reassessed or revised in response to digital challenges. To a surprising degree, humanities scholars have proved reluctant to use digital tools other than word processing programs, online library and archive catalogues, and digital teaching platforms (such as Moodle or Blackboard) and online newspapers or scholarly journals (e.g. through JStor). Few in my own discipline of history count the use of digital tools among their research methodologies.[11] They may search digital archives of texts (such as newspapers) but most still read digital sources "closely" in conventional, tried-and-true ways, without recourse to digital tools

---

[10] Jim Leach, "The Revolutionary Implications of the Digital Humanities," Fifth International Conference of HASTAC, University of Michigan, December 2, 2011: https://www.neh.gov/about/chairman/speeches/the-civilizing-implications-the-digital-humanities. Accessed Febuary 3, 2018.

[11] An alternative explanation is that humanists too often conflate analysis of empirical data, especially by today's social scientists, with the unreflective positivism of many nineteenth century scientists—an epistemological stance they reject. But the field of study that was once called "humanities computing" or "social science history"—much like digital humanities approaches developed more recently—shows few signs of replicating the positivism of the past and often begins instead with the theoretical perspectives and questions of postmodern philosophers. On the use of digital tools in history, see Robert B. Townsend, "Historians and the Technologies of Research," *Perspectives on History* (publication of the American Historical Association), October 2017.

or "distant reading."[12] A close examination of digital archives on Sambuca, also reveals mainly the unfulfilled potential of the digital revolution. While greater use of digital tools and digital data would almost certainly support the exploration of new research questions it would not necessarily require revised answers to older questions. In this paper I demonstrate both the limits and promise of the digital revolution for scholarship on Sambuca.

By comparing research practices before and after the digital revolution, this paper first reinforces Lara Putnam's powerful argument that scholars still need to travel to specific local places if they wish to develop sophisticated analyses of their residents or emigrants.[13] The digital archive is insufficient. Nevertheless, with digital archives expanding daily, scholars should also not ignore their rich opportunities to broaden the knowledge created by earlier scholarship. Digital archives of visual, audio and demographic materials can and should allow scholars to pose new research questions that could scarcely have been imagined forty years ago. They can also extend pre-digital analyses of culture and political economy into the recent past. Finally, this paper identifies at least one opportunity to use digital archives and tools to revisit and revise more fundamentally earlier scholarship. It ends by suggesting that collaborations of scholars and "citizen researchers"[14] descended from Sambuca's emigrants—who use the same digital tools and digital archives—can offer new answers to the research questions of the 1970s and 1980s.

---

[12] Kathryn Schultz, "What is Distant Reading," *New York Times,* June 24, 2011.
[13] Lara Putnam, "The Transnational and the Text-Searchable: Digitized Sources and the Shadows They Cast," *The American Historical Review* 121, 2 (April 2016): 377-402.
[14] For an early use of the term, "citizen researcher" see "What's Going On," *History News* 31, 4 (1976): 82-83 that contrasts "specialists" and "citizen researchers." The term gained traction during the digital revolution, especially with the development of an online research method called "crowdsourcing." See Jeremy Teitelbaum, "Will Crowdsourcing Revolutionize Scholarship?" *UConn Today,* October 25, 2010.

CHOOSING A RESEARCH SITE BEFORE AND AFTER THE
DIGITAL REVOLUTION

Fifty years ago, scholars working in several disciplines simultaneously turned to research in southern Italy's rural areas for clues to economic, political and cultural changes that were then sweeping the so-called "third world" in the aftermath of twentieth-century decolonization. One labor economist even portrayed modern Italy as a "school for awakening countries."[15] Of course, this surge in scholarship on southern Italy cannot explain why *foreign* scholars chose Sambuca di Sicilia as a research site. Comparing the choice of research sites before and after the digital revolution thus provides a first measure of the scholarly impact of technical change.

Forty years ago, scholars began new research by undertaking literature reviews or reading the appropriate historiography, developing research questions, surveying plausible methods and locating useful archives. They continue do so today. In the disciplines of anthropology and history, personal relationships then often determined the choice of research site. Anthropologists had to gain access to a community before they could participate in and observe it or begin to understand it from an insider's perspective. Historians had to identify and gain access to national or local archives (some of them private or "hidden").[16] The digital revolution has not eliminated the importance of personal relationships and communication that create the trust that can open doors to communities and archives, especially in isolated or rural areas. What it has done is to speed the journey along the pathway to the chosen site. The digital revolution has not rendered physical travel redundant or unnecessary.

---

[15] Maurice F. Neufeld, *Italy: School for Awakening Countries; the Italian Labor Movement in its Political, Social, and Economic Setting from 1800 to 1960* (Ithaca: New York State School of Industrial and Labor Relations, Cornell University, 1961).

[16] That collections can remain hidden, inaccessible, and therefore unused remains a problem even in the digital age, see Elizabeth Yakel, "Hidden Collections in Archives and Libraries," *OCLC Systems & Services: International Digital Library Perspectives*, 21, 2 (2005): 95-99. https://doi.org/10.1108/10650750510598675. Accessed April 11, 2018.

A personal example from my own past illustrates both points. By summer 1976, as a graduate student in history at the University of Michigan, I had completed my comprehensive exams after reading widely in U.S. and Italian history, anthropology and interdisciplinary urban studies. I had proposed to write a dissertation that would compare what I called "housing and house life" among Italians living in Italy and as immigrants in the years between 1880 and 1930.[17] My research questions asked about the significance of built environments (houses and constructed urban spaces) for everyday domestic life and neighborhood social relationships as people moved from one place to another. Because earlier studies of Italian immigrants had emphasized Italian familism,[18] I was especially interested in assessing the relative importance of kinship, shared class or occupation and friendship in facilitating cooperation during migration and in the subsequent formation of immigrants' new neighborhood social networks. At the same time no historian of American immigration in the 1970s could ignore the field's central questions, which focused on the relationship of geographical/ spatial and social/ occupational mobility. Did migrants really "move up" as they traveled within and between Italy and America? And was pursuit of personal economic mobility an alternative to collective commitments to leftist peasant or worker movements?

Aware of the importance of *campanilismo*, I was determined my research would respect Italy's well-documented localism. I proposed to compare immigrants from a single Italian town or region--at home and in an American destination where they clustered after migration. My preliminary research led me to Elizabeth Street in Lower Manhattan, where contemporaries had document-

---

[17] I borrowed the analytical concept "house life" from Henry Lewis Morgan, *Houses and House-Life of the American Aborigines* (Washington, D.C.: Government Printing Office, 1881). Morgan may have borrowed it from the German concept of *Wohnweisen*, as used by German ethnologists. My dissertation was titled "Houses and People: Sicilians in Sicily and New York, 1890-1930," Ph.D. University of Michigan, 1979.

[18] Edward Banfield, *The Moral Basis of a Backward Society* (New York: Free Press, 1958); Virginia Yans-McLaughlin, *Family and Community: Italian Immigrants in Buffalo, 1880-1930* (Ithaca: Cornell University Press, 1977).

ed separate clusters of immigrants from the coastal and mountain areas around Palermo and from the region surrounding Sciacca. Once I discovered the published archives of nineteenth-century doctor and folklorist, Giuseppe Pitrè (who had written about house life, proverbs, songs and stories), and had learned of the availability of Pitrè's library and material culture collections in a Palermo museum, I knew I had a workable research design.[19]

The remaining challenge was to locate an accessible local archive somewhere in the home regions of Elizabeth Street's immigrants. Stefano Somogyi's 1971 work on municipal-level demographic data facilitated identification of towns near Palermo and Sciacca with high rates of emigration,[20] while Josef Barton's *Peasants and Strangers*, published in 1975, confirmed that some Sicilian towns had local archives preserving documentation on emigration.[21] When I departed for Sicily in early 1977, more than a dozen towns remained on my list of potential research sites; not one was the subject of a published history, let alone as a book accessible at that time in the United States. Once in Sicily, I first tried without success to talk my way into the municipal archives of several small towns near Palermo. Then, on International Women's Day, March 8, 1977, I met anthropologists Jane and Peter Schneider in the Museo Pitrè in Palermo. Within days, I was in Sambuca (northwest of Sciacca), perusing its archive. A personal connection gave me access, determining my research site.[22]

---

[19] Giuseppe Pitrè, *Biblioteca delle tradizioni popolare*, 22 volumes (Palermo, 1871-1913). As a folklorist, Pitrè may have been familiar with the German ethnologists, see *La famiglia, la casa, la vita del popolo siciliana*, vol. 24, *Biblioteca delle tradizioni popolare*.
[20] Stefano Somogyi, *Bilanci Demografici del Comuni Siciliani dal 1861 al 1961* (Palermo: Università di Palermo, Istituto di Scienze Demografiche, 1971).
[21] Josef Barton, *Peasants and Strangers: Italians, Roumanians, and Slovaks in an American City, 1890-1950* (Cambridge, Mass.: Harvard University Press, 1975). I had not yet read the Schneiders' recent book, *Culture and Political Economy*, which did not, in any case identify Sambuca as their research site because they had followed a disciplinary convention, not shared by historians, of using a pseudonym, Villamaura.
[22] The Schneiders later described to me the more complex net of personal connections that first brought them to Sambuca in the mid 1960s.

Today, a young researcher possessed of the same academic training and interested in the same research questions has many digital tools to speed preparation for research but far fewer to assist in the choice of an appropriate research site. Zotero, JStor, and WorldCat accelerate the creation of extensive bibliographies, even for works published well before 1975.[23] Sorting, alphabetizing, and gaining access to publications listed on bibliographies are more swiftly accomplished today. Many of the scholarly books and articles I consulted in Ann Arbor and New York before traveling to Sicily can now be consulted online without leaving one's home office. Google Books has even digitized some of the most obscure printed sources on nineteenth century rural Sicily (and also on Sambuca)-- in the 1970s these could be read only in Italy.[24]

At the same time, digital tools deliver information in challenging volumes. Do a Google search for "emigration AND Sicily" and decide for yourself how you might begin to survey the 286,000 resulting "hits." Switch to Google Scholar and the number diminishes to "only" 15,000. Fortunately, more focused researchers can now survey and compare from afar the numbers of publications about individual Sicilian towns in the online catalog of Palermo's municipal library. (When I completed that exercise for the towns I had considered as potential research sites in 1976, I discovered that Sambuca would not have risen to the top of the list.) But the digital revolution has only modestly improved access to infor-

---

[23] I'm happy to report that when I completed digital searches for pre-1975 publications recently, I found almost nothing that did not appear in the bibliography I created in 1976 using painstaking, slow, traditional methods. Pre-1975 publications about Sambuca were limited to a fascist-era study of the town's Arab roots, two immediate-postwar studies of local artists (one of them early modern, the other contemporary), and a 1904 study of Sambuca's patron saint, the *SS Maria dell'Udienza*.

[24] Researchers can now read Navarro della Miraglia's *La Nana*, which has been digitized by Google Books. In addition, a Google Book advanced search for "Sambuca Zabut" conducted on February 5, 2018 delivered 3860 hits. A similar search for "Sambuca di Sicilia" delivered 4200 hits. Even Sambuca's local newspaper, *La Voce di Sambuca* is now available in a digitized version on line: http://www.lavocedisambuca.it/archivio-storico/ Accessed April 27, 2018.

mation about Sicily's archives. In 1976 no list of them existed. Today, a researcher can identify a few in rural locations, including Sambuca, on the WorldWideWeb. (Since Sambuca's archive was professionally systematized and moved to a new location only in 1996, its website also provides a completely accurate description of the condition in which I had encountered it in 1977--"preserved on shelves in huge cardboard boxes ... labeled 'Various' and piled on the ground without order.") Nevertheless, the words "emigration" and "emigrants" appear nowhere in the online description of Sambuca's archive.[25] Today's researcher could not, for example, discern whether *fogli di famiglia* and *liste della leva*—vitally important sources for me as I compiled the names and social characteristics of the town's migrants—are accessible there. Travel is still required.

And personal communication will remain a necessary task for researchers in search of research sites. Email can facilitate inquiries made to Sicily's municipal offices but only if a typically harried local clerk finds time to answer. (The web page for Sambuca's archive provides no contact email address.) Scholarly Listservs such as H-Mediterranean, H-Italy, or H-Migration also allow beginning researchers to contact highly specialized researchers for advice, but they must formulate their questions carefully so as not to appear as lazy or uninformed seekers of shortcuts.[26] Even with advantages of speedy emails, the choice of research site will likely be influenced by and established through personal communication. Even today, the researcher cannot remain in her cubicle or home office forever. A journey to Sambuca to explore –and to be surprised by--its archives could no more be avoided in 2018 than in 1977.

---

[25] SIUSA, Sistema Informativo Unificato per la Soprindenza Archivistiche, Comune di Sambuca di Sicilia: http://siusa.archivi.beniculturali.it/cgi-bin/pagina.pl?TipoPag=comparc& Chiave=160966. Accessed February 3, 2018.
[26] I had not contacted Jane and Peter Schneider by post before I traveled to Sicily, largely because I could not know that the "Villamaura" of their recently published book *Culture and Political Economy* was the name of a town—Sambuca—on my list of potential sites.

SAMBUCA'S MANY ARCHIVES:
BEFORE AND AFTER THE DIGITAL REVOLUTION

Once a research site is selected, and the historian is ready to explore archives, the impact of the digital revolution becomes both more significant and more complex. For a researcher with my research questions, multiple archives beckoned for attention. I could explore Sambuca as a physical place—a kind of archive of itself—and meet and talk with people about their relationships and experiences. I could explore Sambuca's chaotic municipal archive and its piles of handwritten documents; I could seek historic photographs of the town. I could expand my scholarly bibliography to include additional publications—from government documents to novels and poetry—that mentioned (usually fleetingly) nineteenth century life in Sambuca. Finally, because researchers in the 1970s and 1980s were especially enthusiastic about immigrants' memories of the past, I could have used oral history and life narrative methods to create a unique memory archive of the town's inhabitants or emigrants.[27]

Because my 1970s research questions focused on the physical and embodied worlds of houses and mobile human bodies, I devoted long research hours in Sambuca to surveying the town's buildings (using as guide a cadaster from the second half of the nineteenth century) and treating the town itself as a physical archive of surviving fragments of an earlier built environment. I devoted even more time to the "reconstitution" of the families of migrants identified in local records. (Eventually I identified 3500 emigrated individuals and compiled demographic data—dates and place of birth, marriage, death, parentage--occupations, and addresses for them in Sambuca and—to a far more limited degree—

---

[27] In the United States, much early oral history work with immigrants was undertaken in Pennsylvania: See John Bodnar, *Anthracite Peoples: Families, Unions, and Work, 1900-1940* (Harrisburg: Pennsylvania Historial and Museum Commission, 1983). In Italy, the oral historical work also focused on workers but in northern cities, while work with southern Italians continued to be dominated by anthropologists. See e.g. Luisa Passerini, *Torino operaia e fascismo: una storia orale*, Vol. 894, Biblioteca di cultura moderna (Roma/Bari: Laterza,1984).

in the United States.[28]) Struggling with the local dialect, my access to Sambuca's memory archive remained limited (although I eventually learned to read dialect, allowing me to access fully Pitrè's collection of proverbs and stories as print archives of peasant subjectivity). Nor could Elizabeth Street offer a rich memory archive of Sambuca's emigrants as most Sambucesi arriving after 1895 had either moved quickly away from Manhattan or traveled directly to Brooklyn; when I began visiting Elizabeth Street in 1976, Chinese immigrants had replaced Sicilians as residents.

In the intervening 40 years, the digital revolution has produced an exciting array of new "digital" or "virtual" archives. To date they have never been used by scholars interested in Sambuca. To inspire greater scholarly use of digital archives, I briefly survey six of them--Wikipedia; the World Wide Web's cornucopia of images and its collections of text-heavy webpages; YouTube; Facebook, and *Ancestry.com*. New scholarly knowledge will likely begin to emerge from these digital archives when scholars begin asking new questions about Sicily in the twenty-first century rather than returning to old questions about the nineteenth or twentieth centuries. Most new knowledge from digital archives will extend or broaden rather than revise pre-digital knowledge. The relentless presentism of most digital archives makes it very unlikely they will have much impact on pre-digital knowledge, which largely focused on the years from 1800 to 1970. Nevertheless, this paper's penultimate section will explore how shared access to *Ancestry.com* might enable scholars and genealogists to revise earlier interpretations of mobility and the relative importance of kinship and friendship offered in my own earlier research.

In 2018, beginning researchers, regardless of their interests, typically initiate a Google Search that leads directly to Wikipedia.

---

[28] Family reconstitution draws on archives—often maintained by religious organizations or states—that preserve anagraphic registries of residents, birth, marriage and death records, military records, *fogli di famiglia*—expired household registry forms in Sambuca from the early twentieth century—and American personal records, too. My discussion of *Ancestry.com* will address the American counterparts of the records in Sambuca's archives.

Wikipedia entries exist for "Sambuca" (the "anise-flavored usually colourless liqueur") and for both "Sambuca di Sicilia" and "Sambuca Zabut." The town's English-language Wikipedia entry locates Sambuca geographically (on a map) and administratively (within the Province of Agrigento, formerly Girgenti). It offers a truncated history that begins with Sambuca's Arab origins and ends with the seventeenth century. For modern Sambuca, this Wikipedia entry notes incoherently only that "in the nineteenth century [it] is rich with culture. In those years it formed an enlightened middle class, which the animator Vincent Navarro was more qualified as a medical time out, writer, poet and patriot."[29] The English-language entry also includes a list of the town's main tourist attractions and its "sister cities," along with links to other webpages, including a Sambuca MySpace page.[30] There is no mention of the history of emigration from the town. Sambuca's Italian language Wikipedia entry is both more up-to-date and richer in its historical description and in its awareness of the town's changing local economy and politics. The entry has been revised quite recently, for it notes that in 2016 Sambuca joined a group of eighteen previously-chosen "villages" among Italy's "Borgo dei Borghi," (a curated list of the country's most beautiful small villages).[31] The Italian-language entry also lists prominent locals and provides worthy websites but it too makes no mention of emigration from Sambuca to other parts of the world. As a first entry into research,

---

[29] https://en.wikipedia.org/wiki/Sambuca_di_Sicilia. Accessed February 4, 2018. I assume the quoted material reflects a poor translation—perhaps with the help of Google Translate—from an Italian language text. Vincenzo Navarro, the father of novelist Emanuele Navarro della Miraglia, was known locally already in the 1970s as instrumental in "animating" local publications and political discussions; he was a part-time doctor and intellectual who relocated from Ribera to escape malaria in Sambuca. The reference to Navarro as a "patriot" calls attention to his support for Italy's Risorgimento and unification. See n. 8.

[30] The reference to MySpace suggests the entry is both old and out of date. Facebook had surpassed MySpace as the most popular social media platform by 2008. See Amy Lee, "MySpace Collapse: How the Social Network Fell Apart," *The Huffington Post*, June 30, 2011.

[31] https://it.wikipedia.org/wiki/Sambuca_di_Sicilia. Accessed February 4, 2018. The *Borgo dei Borghi* competition is discussed in greater detail below.

Wikipedia is not so much inaccurate as it is inadequate. Most researchers would be better advised to begin by reading the pre-digital scholarship noted above.

Visualizing Digital Sambuca

Since my 1970s research had focused on the physical, built environment of Sambuca, it seemed plausible that the digital archive of images compiled on the WorldWideWeb would today offer a valuable resource. There, in fact, a researcher using the Google Image Search tool quickly encounters Sambuca as the distinctive urban form that pre-digital scholars had termed "agrotown."[32] Not perched on a hilltop like other Italian towns, Sambuca descends a long, ridge; in the image archive it appears often with either distant mountains or *Lago Arancio* (a dammed reservoir built between 1949 and 1952) in the foreground or hinterground, emphasizing its rural setting. By contrast, people—images of Sambucesi or others in Sambuca--scarcely appear in the digital archive. A researcher must scroll through almost 400 of over 600 images before finding humans. Surprisingly, both the densely-built agrotown and Sambuca's surrounding countryside appear largely uninhabited and almost empty.

The digital image archive for Sambuca on the WorldWideWeb collects recent photographs, supplemented by a few digitized maps.[33] There are few representations or images of the town created by artists with paintbrushes or computers in hand. The images

---

[32] To be accurate, the scholarly term "agrotown" appears nowhere on the webpages featuring images of Sambuca.

[33] For this paper, I have not included an analysis of Sambuca as it is represented with the digital GoogleMaps or other mapping tools. I can note, however, that I could find no map of the town when I first visited in 1977. I drew by hand a map as I surveyed the town's housing. A cartographer at the Free University of Berlin then transformed my hand-drawn map into the form that appears in *From Sicily to Elizabeth Street*. My ongoing comparison of place names associated with documentation of Sambuca's 3500 migrants suggests that the names of many *cortili* and streets changed, first during the fascist regime and later under the postwar Republic. Furthermore, GoogleMaps currently provides names for fewer than half of the town's *cortili*.

allow Sambuca to be viewed either from a considerable distance or, in close-up photography, as a compilation of some of its many constituent parts, mainly short stretches of streets or grand buildings. What is not easily visible are the town's dwelling houses or residents. In images of the countryside surrounding Sambuca, one sees the cultivation of wine and photos of green vineyards but not the vast, brown and sometimes burned over wheat fields that have characterized Sicily's interior. The wind turbines that a visitor to present-day Sambuca sees on the surrounding hills appear only among the "related images" Google thoughtfully suggests. Images of Sambuca's modern suburb—*la zona di trasferimento*—which is clearly visible and walkable on Google Maps—did not appear in a Google Image search for Sambuca di Sicilia.

Of the many isolated parts that collectively create Sambuca's urbanity, photos of churches, a monastery and a convent appear most often, along with a few buildings constructed by wealthy or baronial former residents and a few public places that currently symbolize either the town's antiquity (archeological sites, ruins of classical columns, a crenellated medieval tower, a fountain), its historical wealth (several palaces in various states of renovation or dilapidation) or its modernity (e.g. the town's small, recently renovated nineteenth-century theater, *L'Idea*, a very recent public sculpture of a snail[34]--discussed further below—the town's municipal offices and a 20th century war monument). A digital photo of a large harp, erected recently at one of town's entry points, also provides a visual reminder of one of several competing explanations offered by residents for the town's much-disputed name.[35] Also pictured in the digital archive are Sambuca's piazzas, streets

---

[34] http://www.sicanitourist.it/portal/index.php/it/galleria/category/6-sambuca-di-sicilia.html. Accessed April 26, 2018.

[35] According to some, the name Sambuca is the romanization of the word for a lyre or harp played throughout *magna Grecia*; others associate the name with a variety of elderberry that grows locally. Still others claim that elder flowers (Sambuca) gave the town its name. Both explanations seek a pre-Arab-conquest origin for the town's name. http://www.tempieterre.it/wp-content/uploads/2013/03/Sambuca-di-Sicilia-Arpa.jpg. Accessed April 26, 2018.

(most often the town's main street or *corso*) and courtyard-like semi-public/semi-domestic spaces that are shared by several families and called *cortili*. (These *cortili* figured prominently in my pre-digital analysis of neighborhood social relationships in Sambuca and their re-creation on Elizabeth Street.)

Again, however, few people appear in the images of streets, piazzas and *cortili*. When one searches for "Sambuca Zabut" rather than "Sambuca di Sicilia" the town's *vicoli Saraceni*, or *sette vaneddi* ("Saracen alleyways" or "seven alleys") rise to the top of Google Search's archive of image thumbnails. For those not satisfied to accept a Greek harp as the source of the town's name, the Saracen alleyways point toward another popular alternative etymology for the town's name—one reaching back to the period of Arab rule of Sicily (831-1091). Wikipedia hedges its bets, noting the possibility both that the town was named after Zabut Al-Arab Emir who built a castle on a nearby mountain or quoting Sicilian novelist Leonardo Sciascia that the Arabic designation, "As-Sambugah" was applied to the current location as a "remote place." Either way, the *vicoli saraceni*, too, are largely devoid of human life in the digital archive.

Digital images of buildings represent Sambuca's past but exclusively in their present-day forms. I found only two historical images of Sambuca in a recent image search. Significantly, I think, both included humans as part of streetscapes. One--an undated, black and white historical postcard, probably from the late 1950s—captures from the middle distance the town's *corso*, main piazza and *Chiesa della Carmine*; the humans on the street are busy and faceless individuals walking swiftly toward unknown destinations.[36] Undated but reaching further back to an earlier Sambuca (1920 or earlier in my estimation) is a second photo centered on a small group of men, barefoot children of various ages and a single black-clad woman. The group stands on rough cobblestones in front of the Chiesa San Giorgio (destroyed around 1958) with the entrance to the *vicoli Saraceni* nearby. Uploaded onto *TripAdvi-*

---

[36] https://i.ytimg.com/vi/2iGJn4Dsnz0/hqdefault.jpg. Accessed April 26, 2018.

sor.com, the photo is captioned, *pare che fosse la moschea* ("it could have been a mosque").[37]

Inhabited dwelling houses are extremely difficult to discern in Sambuca's digital image archive. For that reason alone, it seems unlikely that an analysis of this digital archive could spark revisions of my predigital research findings on nineteenth century houses and houselife. On the other hand, the digital archive could—and should--inspire new questions. Examined alongside YouTube and Facebook archives, for example, researchers could easily ask about the economic and cultural transformation of the town after 1960, as it experienced a second mass migration (and significant numbers of returns as well), recovered from the 1968 earthquake, and responded to Italy's integration into the European Union.

Sambuca's YouTube Archive

In sharp contrast to Sambuca's digital image archive, the digital videos of Sambuca that are viewable on YouTube uniformly position people—as individuals and in groups—more centrally. Researchers are not the audience that individuals intend to reach when they upload videos to YouTube but scholarly Italianists, especially those interested in popular culture, are beginning to analyze them.[38] According to one analysis of global YouTube content, the largest categories for YouTube videos are product reviews, "how-to" videos, Vlogs, gaming videos, comedy videos, "haul" videos (that showcase individuals using products), Memes, "Best of" videos, and educational videos.

Sambuca's YouTube archive—currently represented by about 40,000 short videos—does not quite match this typology. Almost twenty percent of Sambuca YouTube videos were uploaded by provincial and national television producers and local radio (e.g. Radio Zabut) to enhance access to local news and weather reports.

---

[37] An assertion I am unable to evaluate, given my limited knowledge of the history of sacral architecture. See https://media-cdn.tripadvisor.com/media/ photos/0e/50/63/e0/l-antica-chiesa-di-san.jpg. Accessed April 26, 2018.
[38] See for example Ilaria Serra, "Teaching Italy Through its Music; The Meaning of Music in Italian Cultural History," *Italica* 88, 1 (Spring 2011): 94-114.

In these videos, exceptional events are documented. (The same pattern can be seen in more personal videos. When it snows in Sambuca --as it does occasionally--a new video of snow-covered streets or buildings inevitably appears.) There are numerous digital news reports about mafia arrests in Sambuca in 2016. In a more educational upload by an individual, a video records the talk given by a Sambuca-origin specialist at a local oncology conference focusing on breast and colon cancers.[39]

By far the largest category of videos about Sambuca—well over half--use documentarian formats to promote the town as a tourist destination. Sambuca itself becomes a product for review and purchase in these videos. Whether promotional or celebratory and "boosting," these videos apparently function as contemporary expressions of Sambucesi's well-documented pride in their hometown and in its continuing reputation as a site of artistic and literary production. At the same time, the videos serve as searchable promotions of commercial tourism, something that has become more important to the town economy with Italy's integration into the European Union. The digital archive thus shifts attention away from the peasant culture that was the focus of pre-digital scholarship, toward commercial culture. Another 20 percent of Sambuca's YouTube videos are straightforward advertisements, produced by local restaurants, hotels, and B&Bs or by realtors interested in renting or selling residential properties portrayed as attractive vacation homes.[40]

Many promotional videos in the Sambuca YouTube archive feature local folk customs and culture, making them a rich resource for researchers in folklore and cultural studies and their place in contemporary campaigns to promote the commerce of tourism.[41] Videos, often with music, capture key moments--the

---

[39] https://www.youtube.com/watch?v=JkvPibvJ-mA. Accessed April 26, 2018.
[40] As an example, see this B&B advertisement: https://www.youtube.com/watch?v=X83yzMYMIFc. Accessed April 26, 2018.
[41] The same is undoubtedly true for film studies researcher but since I know less about that field, I do not speculate on what such scholars will find compelling about Sambuca's YouTube archive of videos.

procession, the evening fireworks, the neon-lighted streets and sense of crowds and excitement—in the town's festival for its patron saint, the *SS Maria dell'Udienza*, held each year in May.[42] Sambuca's Carnival celebrations are also well documented and could easily be compared to the fictional Carnival scene evoked by Emanuele Navarro della Miraglia in his nineteenth century novel *La Nana*.[43] One video focuses on a troupe of children and youthful Sambucesi parading and dancing through the streets dressed as cowboys and Indians.[44] (Surprisingly, however, one finds no Carnival revelers dressed as Saracens or Arabs.) Some video titles identify themselves straightforwardly as folkloric and explicitly seek viewers with interests in folklore as entertainment for tourists. Apparently, too, new festivals are now regularly mounted and documented on video. Several celebrate food. Of these only snail eating had a place in pre-digital archives, e.g. the proverb, "*Sammucari, babbaluci*" from Pitrè's nineteenth century collection.[45] (Sambuca even celebrated the unveiling of an attractive snail figurine as public art in 2014.[46]) Sambuca now also claims *minni di vergini* ("virgins' breasts," a pastry traditionally manufactured by nuns) as a local speciality, also celebrated with its own festival.[47] With the collapse of the USSR and the reorientation of Italy's Communist Party after 1989, competition emerged for Sambuca's once-lively May Day; beginning in 2013, Sambuca's youth sponsored a festival which prominently featured a popular music con-

---

[42] https://www.youtube.com/watch?v=WpLNAMiMS-Y. Accessed February 4, 2018.
[43] https://www.youtube.com/watch?v=BSbSLASIUDM. Accessed February 4, 2018.
[44] https://www.youtube.com/watch?v=E-SKhD9K1Tk. Accessed February 4, 2018.
[45] Pitrè, *Proverbi*, vol. III, 163.
[46] https://www.youtube.com/watch?v=vBt7RbqfAD8. For a travel blog report on the unveiling of the *lumacha* written by an American tourist and visitor whose grandfather originated in the town (he includes his family tree and history in the blog), see: Matt Maggio, "Babbaluci Festival," http://mattmaggio.com/ page/2/. The snail resonates powerfully with the symbol of Italy's Slow Food Movement, of course; the movement in the United States also hosts an annual "Snail of Approval" celebration for food businesses that honor its principles: https://www. slowfoodusa.org/event/2016-snail-of-approval-celebration. All URLS accessed February 4, 2018.
[47] https://www.youtube.com/watch?v=mIIEkBwkC3g. Accessed February 5, 2018.

cert rather than the red flags, drums and festival atmosphere that had characterized the *Festa dell'Unità* on May 1.

In the 1970s, few tourists had ventured to Sambuca and the town had no tourist infrastructure; there were cafes but no hotels or restaurants (aside from a pizzeria at Lago Arancia).[48] The only visitors I observed there were returning migrants with kin in the town and — of course--the occasional visiting scholar. (I suspect but cannot prove that You Tube videos of Easter time worshipers emerging yearly from mass at the *Chiesa della Carmine*, may, like some of the festival videos, too, find an audience among expatriates.[49]) Thus, scholars interested in how state, capitalist enterprise and culture entwined to develop tourism as an growing concern of rural Sicily will find much of interest in Sambuca's YouTube archive. As part of a still-united Europe, rural Sicily today is not only better integrated into Europe's prosperous economy, its inhabitants appear on YouTube as better dressed, more prosperous and more articulate than they were forty years ago. Recent images on YouTube also reveal that damage from the 1968 earthquake has finally been cleared away. More of the town is whitewashed and plastered; more streets leading into and within the town are paved. Such changes, begun under a Communist municipal government, built the foundation for Sambuca's promotion of tourism.

Tourism campaigns emanating from the Tourism Council of the *Associazione Nazionale Comuni Italiani* (ANCI), a group that initiated its *Borghi più belli d'Italia* in 2001, certainly intensified Sambuca's growing interest in tourism.[50] After its founding four years later, Sambuca's *Pro Loco* became the sponsor of festivals, exhibitions, festas, conferences and concerts.[51] When Sambuca achieved the status of *Borgo dei Borghi* in 2016, the uploading of promotional

---

[48] Arriving earlier than my expected host in the summer of 1980, I found their house locked, so I slept overnight under a bush in the public garden.
[49] https://www.youtube.com/watch?v=Ey06X15DCpY. Accessed February 4, 2018.
[50] Sambuca has had a *ProLoco,* named for its countryside and lake (Adragna, Carboi) since the early 1980s.
[51] The old and new governing documents of the *ProLoco* can be read on line: https://www.prolocosambuca.it/la-pro-loco/statuto/. Accessed April 29, 2018.

videos to YouTube again accelerated. Sambuca also benefited from a follow-up AirBnB campaign managed by a young American of Sicilian descent. At its launch, Sambuca's vice- mayor, the architect Giuseppe Cacioppo, emphasized the exceptional beauty and social cohesion of the Sambuca community which he attributed to a strong culture of hospitality rooted in the town's Arab origins.[52] On YouTube, too, the town's Arab origin seems especially noteworthy when promoting tourism.

The *Borghi più belli d'Italia* initiative reinforced Sambucesi's pre-existing and quite powerful sense of their town as possessed of a unique cultural history and patrimony. YouTube videos now lovingly examine the recently renovated *Teatro L'Idea* and advertise performances held there. Also documented on YouTube are the organization of events by Sambuca's *Forno Sociale* and the local tourist office, the *Pro Loco L'Araba Fenicia*.[53] Recent events have included book launches and discussions, art and textile exhibitions (featuring the well known local artist Giambecchina as well as lesser known artists, including one "naturalized" French Sambucese), and even a conference, the *Festival Folklore Internazionale,* held in 2014.[54] Each year the town also hosts an international poetry prize named after the nineteenth century writer, Navarro della Miraglia.

Searches for videos specifically mentioning "Sambuca Zabut" provide further confirmation that exoticism associated with Arab origin has become an important, if complex, element in tourism promotion. Most of the YouTube videos aimed to capture the eye of potential European or American tourists. Produced in multiple languages (English, French, Spanish, German), they feature Sambuca's *vicoli Saraceni*. (The alleyways were also the site of the

---

[52] "Turismo: Sambuca da Borgo dei Borghi a star di Airbnb," *ANSA*, October 9, 2017. http://www.ansa.it/sicilia/notizie/2017/10/09/turismo-sambuca-da-borgo-dei-borghi-a-star-di-airbnb_ade3445f-a774-4ccc-87ce-263f3d0bf144.html. Accessed February 6, 2018.

[53] Documentation of early events, 2005-2010, is not available; after 2011 (when it sponsored 5 events), cultural programming doubled and continued to grow as Sambuca sought status as *borgo dei borghi*. https://www.prolocosambuca.it/eventi/. Accessed April 29, 2018.

[54] https://www.youtube.com/watch?v=n6YGnLRccEA. Accessed February 7, 2018.

homes offered for sale for a single Euro in a recent campaign aimed at tourists, who were imagined simultaneously as participants in and an audience for local cultural events as described above.) Several videos document how brightly-colored patterned tiles, Arabic calligraphy (translated as "Casa Limone"), the names of Bed and Breakfast establishments (*le Stanze Emir*), tiny windows in blank stone walls, and the color blue distinguish recently renovated *cortile* houses. Renovated BnBs adjoin some of the tiniest and often still-unrenovated peasant dwellings of the type I discussed in my 1970s dissertation. Indeed, videos of the *vicoli Saraceni* provide some of the only places in the YouTube archive where the viewer senses the presence of human habitation. But even there, one sees few plants, no drying laundry, and no open windows through which human beings might peek out to satisfy their curiosity about the videographer lurking outside (a common enough experience when I made photographs or simply wandered into a *cortile* in the 1970s). Does the town mean to suggest with such videos that tourists can safely and completely occupy space without close contact with the town's residents? That they can have "old Sambuca" to themselves now that the Sambucesi have moved to the nearby suburb? That is one possibility. Another is they show no people because they respect privacy or fail to ask permission to display images to the wider public.

For the historian interested mainly in the rural, Sicilian past, the YouTube archive offers little. Videos about both Sambuca di Sicilia and Sambuca Zabut are recent productions, the oldest having been uploaded in 2007. In videos, physical remnants or reproductions of Sambuca's past have been transformed either into folklore or into art for performance and display.[55] Still, one unknown person did compile and digitize (undated) older postcards of Sambuca, flipping through them to create the sensation of the passage of (not

---

[55] https://www.youtube.com/watch?v=nY9r-PsS52s. Accessed February 4, 2018. A local group of young persons called the Associazione Futura Sambuca was exceptional in celebrating the town's past with this simple video about the local, eighteenth-century painter Fra Felice.

strictly chronological) time through the magic of video.[56] Online television and online video newspaper reports also commemorate with film, Powerpoints and older photos the 1968 earthquake that destroyed parts of Sambuca and other towns in the Belice Valley,[57] an event that any historian of Sambuca's recent cultural and political economic transformations would want to analyze in detail to understand its impact. For the historian or anthropologist interested in how the postwar migrations, Italy's economic miracle, and the formation of an integrated Europe has reshaped rural Sicily, attention to YouTube and its promotional and celebratory videos could support a welcome extension of earlier research, reminding readers that the culture and political economy of the Sicilian countryside has continued to change into our own times.

Sambuca in the Facebook Archive: More of the Same?
Viewers have rarely responded with comments to the videos about Sambuca as YouTube allows, suggesting at least some level of local disinterest in them. By contrast, pages created on Facebook exist mainly to facilitate discussion and interaction. Not all succeed of course. There are currently one hundred individual Facebook pages focused on Sambuca. The largest number was created by local businesses; others represent the digital, public face of local organizations like the *Pro Loco Araba Fenicia* or Sambuca's municipal government. Most Facebook pages created by businesses in Sambuca attract very little use or commentary from "friends." But Facebook Groups—there are thirty of them—are somewhat livelier. Two of the three largest Facebook Groups—*Sambuca di Sicilia, Borgo dei Borghi* (with 3000 members) and *Sambuca Borgo Più Bello d'Italia* (with 800 members) both have names that suggest origins in the same nexus of local pride and tourism promotion evident on YouTube. (The 1800-member Group "*Sei di*

---

[56] https://www.youtube.com/watch?v=2iGJn4Dsnz0. Accessed February 4, 2018.
[57] http://www.rainews.it/dl/rainews/articoli/sicilia-ricorda-dramma-belice-50-anni-dopo-terremoto-f182356d-d9a3-4876-bc8c-26b553b89138.html. Accessed February 4, 2018.

Sambuca se...." is not so easily characterized.)⁵⁸ All three Groups were created in the years between 2014 and 2016, as the town's campaign for recognition as a beautiful tourist site peaked. The administrator of *Sambuca di Sicilia, Borgo dei Borghi* launched that group with an inspirational reference to the campaign, proposing as motto "a group that shares a common goal can achieve the impossible."⁵⁹ Given these origins, it is unsurprising that all three Facebook Groups regularly promote the same local events that are documented in the YouTube Archive.

Although rich in embedded photographs (and occasional videos), these three large Facebook Groups also offer more to the interested researcher. For one thing, they document modern Sambucesi speaking and writing in their own voices. After a century of expanding public education in Sicily, it is striking how often they choose to speak and write in dialect—a likely indicator of how effectively social media sites promote a sense of intimacy even in a decidedly public virtual space. A very popular 2014 thread on *Sambuca di Sicilia, Borgo dei Borghi* invited people to post a favorite *ingiuria (sopranome* or nickname) that was used locally. Eleven hundred people responded and the thread created a catalog of modern dialect terms that is in every respect comparable to the nineteenth century collection of proverbs made by folklorist Giuseppe Pitrè.⁶⁰

Although the most common postings on all three Sambuca Facebook Groups feature present-day matters (e.g. the illegal dumping of garbage or news stories of local and provincial interest), individual members also occasionally digitize and post private, presumably family, photos. A researcher can view photos of school classes of children or of earlier municipal events such as a 1985 dis-

---

⁵⁸ "You know you are (or are from…), if…" became a popular meme for Facebook groups around 2009 or 2010. The same meme emerged on YouTube, Pinterest and other social media sites.
⁵⁹ Had someone told me in 1977 that Sambuca would in the future gain recognition as one of the most beautiful villages of Italy, I too probably would have declared that future "impossible."
⁶⁰ https://www.facebook.com/photo.php?fbid=610656815682838&set=gm.79810 34 73553019&type=3&theater. Accessed April 11, 2018.

cussion of *Cantastorie*. One photo evoked memories of the local cinema of the 1950s and tales of its well-known projectionist. Historical postcards have also been posted, including a pre-1920 photo of an animal fair held outside the town and boys (apparently from the 1950s) cavorting near the nearby remains of an ancient Roman aqueduct.[61] (As is typical on Facebook, other group members then "like" or sometimes comment on the photos; "beautiful" is the most common, if not particularly enlightening, response.) Local intellectuals, including those cited in n. 9, above, also regularly introduce perspectives from history (especially the history of Italian and Sambuca-origin leftists, labor activists and anti-fascists) or folklore.

Still, the most common post by Sambucesi on Sambuca's Facebook Groups takes the form of a virtual greeting sent to other members, especially in the days around the Christmas, New Year's and Easter holidays. Many Sambucesi use Facebook to say an occasional exuberant "good morning to everyone," to call attention to the beauty of the nearby lake or the weather on any given day or simply to send *saluti* to an acquaintance who has posted news or photos.[62] Sociability and interaction is considerably more intense than on YouTube and suggest that anthropologists interested in "netnography" (the term for digital ethnography conducted on the WorldWideWeb) could easily extend earlier analyses of local culture and social relations into the twenty-first century[63] To my

---

[61] The best archive of digitized postcards of Sambuca is found on Ebay where, however, images of Sambuca di Sicilia are outnumbered many times over by images of Sambuca Pistoiese https://www.ebay.com/sch/i.html?_from=R40&_trksid=p2053587.m570.l1313.TR12.TRC2.A0.H0.XSambuca+postcards.TRS0&_nkw=Sambuca+postcards&_sacat=0. Accessed April 27, 2018.

[62] Having found me recently on Facebook, the daughter of one of my neighbors in Sambuca in 1982 now sends simple greetings, accompanied by an occasional picture, roughly six to ten times a year. This dedication through small and repeated acts to the maintenance of relationships also figured in the pre-digital research on friendship by Jane and Peter Schneider.

[63] Robert Kozinets, *Netnography: Doing Ethnographic Research Online* (Thousand Oaks, CA: Sage Publications, 2009)

knowledge, however, no researcher has attempted such an exercise for any town in rural Sicily.[64]

While the town's history of mobility is scarcely a major theme in the digital archive of the three Sambuca Facebook Groups, it is modestly more visible than in Wikipedia, digital images or YouTube. Sambucesi have, for example, debated the value of the immigrants who began appearing in Sicily already in the 1970s. Emigration is remembered indirectly through occasional posts in English on the Sambuca Facebook Group pages and my very cursory survey of the three groups' members suggests also that at least a few live elsewhere in Italy, in Europe or in South or (especially) North America. In early 2017, a member alerted Sambucesi to a new Facebook page dedicated to "Sicilians Across the Globe"; that page featured a dialect poem (and image of a snail) highlighting *la babbalucia sammucara sarripara*.[65] Later in the same year, a local intellectual posted a series of photos of monuments and public art to inform Sambucesi that other Italian towns had commemorated their emigrants departed for the Americas. He clearly hoped Sambuca, too, might host an event dedicated to the Sambucesi scattered about Italy, Europe and overseas. An apparently random picture of New York's Verrazano Bridge was posted soon thereafter. Later, a member of the group posted an historical image of men in Argentina sending greetings to their friends at home; it and an ad for a restaurant in Greenwood Village, Colorado, received no feedback. In short, the digital archive created on Facebook is unlikely to provoke major revisions of answers to research questions about migration. It could however find a central place in new analysis of the transformation of Sambuca's earlier peasant economy and culture into a culture and economy revolving around folkloricized rural tourism,

---

[64] But for one corner of the south Italian diaspora, see Donald Tricarico, "Bellas and Fellas in Cyberspace: Mobilizing Italian Ethnicity for Online Youth Culture," *Italian American Review* 1, 1 (January 2011): 1-34

[65] https://www.facebook.com/SiciliansAcrossTheGlobe. Accessed April 25, 2018.

food and wine production (Planeta is an important local brand[66]) and forms of "high" culture represented by scholarship, literary production and art. However such research would not likely change any of answers I offered to my research questions about emigration and the town's emigrants in the 1970s.

Sambuca Webpages and Websites

As the balance of digital text to digital images (still or moving) shifts toward text, as it does on most Worldwide Websites, the possibility of finding new perspectives on the past improves, especially when the researcher begins by searching specifically for webpages that, like my pre-digital scholarship, focus on emigration from Sambuca and immigration of Sambucesi to the United States. Table 1 shows how differing search terms and Boolean searches highlight digital knowledge production that is thematically close to the research questions pre-digital scholarship. While Table 1 confirms again that a clear, anise-flavoured liqueur from central Italy dominates digital knowledge about "Sambuca," knowledge emerging from YouTube, image, and Facebook archives also re-occur in long-form Webpage texts. Searches that link Sambuca to "emigration" or "immigration" generate smaller archives but the Google Analytics tool routinely ranks genealogy and scholarship on Sambuca among the most relevant Websites and displays them at the head of the list of URLs it delivers in response.

---

[66] https://www.tripadvisor.ca/Attraction_Review-g2533492-d2360796-Reviews-Visite_in_Cantina_Planeta-Sambuca_di_Sicilia_Province_of_Agrigento_Sicily.Html. Accessed April 28, 2018.

TABLE 1: Number and Topics of Webpage "Hits" Generated by Google Search Analytics

Search Term/s	Number Webpages indexed	Topic, Top 20 Webpages
Sambuca	4.83 million	Food and drink: business and commerce
Sambuca AND emigration	42,000	Scholarship; hotels
Sambuca AND immigration	99,000	Scholarship, genealogy
"Sambuca di Sicilia"	553,000	Tourism
"Sambuca di Sicilia" AND emigration	12,700	Hotels, genealogy
"Sambuca di Sicilia" AND immigration	2,850	Scholarship, genealogy
"Sambuca Zabut"	27,900	Genealogy, tourism
"Sambuca Zabut" AND emigration	533	Genealogy
"Sambuca Zabut" AND immigration	593	Genealogy, Scholarship

Neither genealogists nor scholars might have anticipated the close association of their two fields of endeavor. According to Jacqueline Jones, a former president of the American Historical Association, historians "have a somewhat uneasy relationship to genealogists. We jump back in time and write a story that largely depends on a linear narrative.... In contrast, genealogists start in the present and then work backwards."[67] Jones concludes that

---

[67] Jacqueline Jones, "A Historian among Genealogists: Working on Who Do You Think You Are?" *Perspectives on History (The News Magazine of the American Historical Association)*, January, 2013. The article describes Jones's experience working as consultant and "talking head" for the BBC show "Who Do You Think You Are?" (a program for which I have also consulted). She views the experience as

scholars and genealogists can coexist in harmony, but her recommendation for coexistence acknowledges that harmony has not been the norm. Similarly, citizen researchers--whether they consider themselves to be family historians or genealogists--are suspicious of scholars. Responding to an online "defence" of family history in 2011, one argued "the problem with historians is obvious, they spend a lot of time up [among?] themselves. Historians, like a lot of 'professionals,' also do not like having their toes trodden on. Trust me...I see it in every meeting I attend. Everything is history, including families and if some historians fail to see that then they are not historians, they are bean counters." In a conciliatory voice not unlike the one adopted by Jones, a commentator with the screenname Dermaptera, disagreed mildly, asserting "I don't think 'academic historians' are as sniffy about family history now as they used to be."[68] Google Analytics may see historians and citizen researchers as bedfellows in the digital archive, but both groups worry about the coupling. Citizen researchers are reluctant to accept the authority of those they call "academic historians" or "professionals" (in scare quotes), while professional historians sometimes "scoff" at genealogists who "are busy spitting into DNA-collection tubes ... and tracing their family history back as far as they can."[69]

Although Jones believed it was genealogists whose "currency is demographic information—names, birth and death dates, and marriages," I have already insisted on the centrality of the same type of "demographic" information from Sambuca's archive for answering my 1970s research questions about social relationships among mi-

---

learning firsthand "about the fascinating intersection of entertainment, commerce, genealogy, and historical scholarship" in popular television production.

[68] Alison Light, "In Defence of Family History," *The Guardian*, September 11, 2014. https://www.theguardian.com/books/2014/oct/11/genealogy-not-historys-poor-relation-family. Accessed April 28, 2018.

[69] John Sedgwick, "The Historians Versus the Genealogists," *New York Times*, April 12, 2018. In this piece Sedgwick notes his growing enthusiasm (and respect) for the methods of genealogy after discovering that one of his own ancestors was central to scholarly research that he did not initially know was related to his family's past.

grants.[70] In fact, in the 1980s as I tried with the primitive SOUNDEX census index to identify Sambucesi in the microfilmed census records of Louisiana, Illinois, and New York—a necessary step as I sought to assess the social and occupational mobility of immigrants from Sambuca in the United States--I usually found myself seated among and completely outnumbered by genealogists and family historians in the New York Public Library's Local History and Genealogy room or in the microfilm reading room of the National Archives in Washington.[71] The digital revolution has wrought profound changes in the research practices of citizen researchers, especially genealogists, while professional scholars working with individual-level information (sometimes called microdata when it is delivered digitally) have responded more slowly. The digital revolution has speeded the identification of individuals across dispersed document series created in far-flung locations. It has facilitated extensive communication and collaboration among genealogists. It could support expanded collaboration between citizen researchers and professional historians if both could overcome their mutual distrust.

The digital archive of Websites featuring Sambuca's "emigrants" (who were of course labeled as "immigrants" in the United States) points to several types of new digital knowledge production. They introduce the research interests and practices among Sambuca-origin citizen researchers and point toward possible paths to the reconciliation with professional historians that both Jones and Dermaptera advocate. Below I distinguish among digital dissemination

---

[70] Demographic historians also use such information or data, albeit more often as "bean counters" using quantitative methods. See, for example, the creation of massive collections of U.S. and global census data that began as an initiative of demographic historians at the University of Minnesota but that removed all nominal identifiers when doing so: https://usa.ipums.org/usa/; https://international.ipums.org/international/. Only the North Atlantic Population Project (NAPP: https://www.nappdata.org/napp/) allows individual level searches by surname. All sites accessed April 29, 2018.

[71] For the U.S. Census Bureau's description of SOUNDEX, see https://www.census.gov/history/www/genealogy/decennial_census_records/soundex_1.html. Accessed April 27, 2018.

of *family histories*, digital *archives of demographic documents* (that support both genealogists's production of digital family trees[72] and scholarly transAtlantic record linkage) and, digital *platforms for communication and sharing* among researchers.[73] I also briefly examine a website "Sambuca Club" as an extraordinary example of how one passionate and hard-working citizen researcher mobilized collaborative efforts among genealogists to integrate all three genres of digital knowledge production under a single URL umbrella.

If Alison Smith is correct that "After shopping and porn, family history is the most popular activity on the web,"[74] then Sambuca-origin citizen researchers lag far behind others. Among the top-ranked webpages described in Table 1, I found only two family history narratives, both focused on a single Sambuca-origin family. The first provides a short account of the "Scalisi, Abbate, Di Benedetto and Allotta Families" written in 2016 (and accompanied by several very high-quality photos) and included in a genealogy project titled "Immigration Histories of Rockford" (Illinois), sponsored by the Culture and Education Committee of the Greater Rockford Italian American Association.[75] Rockford was an important site of secondary settlement for the peasants from Sambuca who first traveled to Louisiana between 1890 and 1910 in order to work in sugar cultivation and harvesting, a story recounted in my book *Militants*

---

[72] For those who do not recognize the family tree as a genre for reporting research, a visually clear explanation is provided here: https://www.smartdraw.com/family-tree/. Accessed April 29, 2018.

[73] Given the popularity of oral history methods in the United States since the 1970s, I was surprised my Google Search generated few digitized Webpages with oral histories of Sambuca-origin immigrants. Instead, I found another genre that may be worth further exploration—the "tourist memoir" written by Sambuca-origin citizen researchers who travel to Sambuca and document their experiences there. For one particularly full and thoughtful example see Robbie Tiffany Mantooth, "Travels in Sicily," December 21, 2011. https://issuu.com/travels_in_italy/docs/pdf_journal. Accessed April 29, 2018. I discuss what scholars call "heritage tourism" in greater detail below.

[74] In her "Defence of Family History," https://www.theguardian.com/books/2014/oct/11/genealogy-not-historys-poor-relation-family. Accessed April 26, 2018.

[75] http://griaa.org/wp-content/uploads/2017/06/Scalisi-Abbate-DiBenedetto-Allotta.pdf. Accessed April 27, 2018.

and Migrants. That book contrasted the modest occupational mobility of Sambuca emigrants of peasant origins to the rapid embrace of education and professional work among the town's upwardly mobile artisans who settled in the New York area, especially in Brooklyn.

Written by one of the great-grandsons of a young girl named Rosalia Abbate (who in 1900 emigrated at age seven with her parents from Sambuca to Louisiana), the Webpage narrative traces the family's residential and occupational moves across several generations. The family history confirms that access to American higher education for this peasant-origin family came only in the 1960s among the third-generation, i.e. the grandchildren, of Rosalia Abbate's family. The pursuit of higher-level occupations by the newly educated in turn scattered them more widely geographically; university educated family members also tended to marry outside their ethnic group.[76] In a fascinating extension of Marcus Lee Hansen's theory of "third generation return," the author of the narrative (whose mother was Danish-American) returned from his home in Colorado to visit his Sicilian grandparents in Rockford every summer, where he became interested already as child in his family's "roots."[77]

A second, closely related webpage provides a powerful example of transnational "roots-seeking" by a youthful, fourth-generation member of the same Rockford family. Published in Sambuca's newspaper *La Voce* and written in Italian by the local architect who as Sambuca's vice mayor has been active in promoting tourism, "Un americano sulla rotta dei bisnonni" recounts how a very tall, six-foot-five young man taught himself Sicilian dialect, visited Sambuca many times and enjoyed a reunion with his great-grandmo-ther's relatives in Sambuca (and also with Scalisi relatives in nearby Bisaquino). The article describes the young man as declaring he now wished also to find a wife from the town. For Sicilian readers, this story of return to Sambuca undoubtedly reinforced the local dis-

---

[76] On the relationship of educational achievement, upward mobility, and spatial scattering, see Christa Wirth, *Memories of Belonging: Descendants of Italian Migrants to the United States, 1884-Present* (Leiden: Brill Academic Publishers, 2015).
[77] Marcus Lee Hansen, "The Problem of the Third Generation Immigrant" (Rock Island, Illinois: Augustana Historical Society, 1938).

course promoting tourism; both hinted at possibilities for what scholars now call "heritage tourism."[78] Roughly translated into English, the *La Voce* story is now also accessible on the "Club Sambuca" webpage. For English-speaking Italian American readers, it instead provides confirmation of continuing family solidarity in the face of spatial and occupational mobility as well as a dramatic evidence of the kind of quirky but ultimately successful passion that drives the individual "quests" many Americans enjoy reading about.[79]

The Abbate family story also illustrates the almost total separation of knowledge production by citizen researchers and professional historians. When I checked, I quickly found the father of Rosalia Abbate among the 3500 migrants I had identified in the 1970s in Sambuca's archive.[80] Since I had no access to family stories when assessing the American mobility of Sambuca's migrants, it is possible that a compilation of them might require me to revise the interpretations generated thirty years ago. Currently, however, the digital revolution has not produced a sizeable archive of Sambuca family narratives. I can still more easily find Sambuca family histories in traditional print publications, such as the one published by the Greater Rockford Italian American Association [81] or in the writings of well-known feminist author Sandra Gilbert

---

[78] Deepak Chhabra, Robert Healy, and Erin Sills, "Staged Authenticity and Heritage Tourism," *Annals of Tourism Research* 30, 3 (July 2003): 702-719.

[79] *La Voce di Sambuca*, June/July, 2004. http://www.lavocedisambuca.it/wp/wp-content/uploads/2016/03/N.392-Giugno-Luglio-2004.pdf. Accessed April 28, 2018. See the English-language version: https://sites.google.com/site/sambucadisicilia/Home/links-to-rockford-il-sambucesi/the-story-of-michele-scalisi. Accessed February 12, 2018.

[80] Admittedly, I knew little about him beyond birthdate, names of parents, an early address and occupation in Sambuca, and the fact that Sambuca's clerks had listed him as living in America in 1931. Still, that is more than his great-great grandson had been able to learn of him, at least as evidenced in the digitized family history narrative.

[81] *Immigration Histories of Rockford Italian Families* (Rockford: Greater Rockford Italian American Association, 2016). Not all Italian families documented in the book are from Sambuca.

whose Brooklyn ancestors included one of Sambuca's midwives.[82] Despite the ubiquity of references to my books about Sambuca in Google's digital archive of Webpages, furthermore, citizen researchers rarely consult them. A single typed letter delivered to my home by the U.S. Postal Service in 2001 and written by retired lawyer Nick Gagliano still constitutes the only communication I have ever received from a Sambuca-origin citizen researcher.[83]

Family history narratives like Rosalia Abbate's are dwarfed in number by the Google Search archive of hundreds of pages that document Sambuca-origin genealogists seeking to locate documents recording their ancestors' births, marriages, military service, work, migrations, naturalizations, and deaths. "Roots-seeking" in pre-digital archives was evident already in the 1970s when I was in Sicily--a product of the so-called "white ethnic" revival in the United States and the publication of Alex Haley's enormously popular African-American family saga, *Roots*.[84] (Soon after the publication of *Roots*, a municipal clerk in a town not far from Sambuca mocked the inquiries he was receiving from the United States and joked that, when asked to provide them a copy of a birth record, he "told them their grandfather was a priest.")[85]

For root-seeking genealogists, along with historians who use the same sources, the impact of the digital revolution has in fact been revolutionary. Unfortunately, that revolution has not built bridges over the chasm that separates the two clusters of research-

---

[82] "Mysteries of the Hyphen: Poetry, Pasta, and Identity Politics," in *Breaking Open: Reflections on Italian-American Writers*, ed. Mary Ann Vigilante-Mannino and Justin Vitiello (West Lafayette, IN: Purdue University Press, 2003); see also Gilbert's introduction to the novel by Tina De Rosa, *Paper Fish* (Chicago: The Wine Press, 1980).

[83] By contrast, I have received over the years at least a dozen queries from persons whose ancestors had lived on Elizabeth Street. The author of the 2001 query about Sambuca—Nick Gagliano, a retired lawyer from Metairie, Lousiana—shared a fifty-page oral family history. I discuss my relationship with Nick in greater detail below.

[84] On the white ethnic revival, see Michael Novak, *The Rise of the Unmeltable Ethnics: Politics and Culture in American Life* (New York: The MacMillan Company, 1972); Alex Haley, *Roots: The Sage of an American Family* (New York: Doubleday, 1977).

[85] Donna Gabaccia, unpublished Field notes, July, 1980.

ers with interests in Sambuca and its emigrants. The scope of this paper does not permit a full accounting of how *Ancestry.com*—founded in 1996 during the headiest, early days of the WorldwideWeb--came to dominate the delivery (for fees) of digitized documents to today's citizen and professional researchers.[86] *Ancestry.com* currently offers 20 billion fully searchable digitized records from 80 different countries to 3 million paying subscribers; it claims to host 100 million family trees and to have collected DNA samples from 10 million persons.[87] As an *Ancestry.com* subscriber, I can assess only in very primitive ways the numbers of Sambuca-origin genealogists using the site because searching Ancestry's collections by the location of a document's creation is almost impossible. Nevertheless, *Ancestry.com's* message boards include over 400 messages referencing Sambuca, the earliest from 2003. A simple keyword search also reveals over 7600 references to Sambuca in the "Public Member Trees." Rockford, Chicago, and Brooklyn predictably appear most frequently in the Public Member Trees. While some trees are complex compilations which include PDF files from the researcher's family archive of photos and documents as well as copies of Ancestry documents (birth, death and marriage records, passenger arrival records, naturalization records, military records, gravesite identifications etc.) most Sambuca-origin family trees are extremely rudimentary. Searching a small sample of about 100 individuals from 50 families in my pre-digital research files led to only 15 family trees. Many of these contain "false positive" identifications because beginning genealogists often do not understand how commonly names are shared in Sicilian families; some prove themselves too impatient to learn how to distinguish one "Audenzio Maniscalco" from dozens of others with the same name. (*Ancestry.com* developers offer what they call an "AncestryAcademy" that calls attention to this chal-

---

[86] A Wikipedia entry for Ancestry exists, of course, but I am unable to assess fully its usefulness without doing considerable original research. See https://en.wikipedia.org/wiki/Ancestry.com. Accessed April 28, 2018.

[87] https://www.ancestry.com/corporate/about-ancestry/company-facts. Accessed April 29, 2018.

lenge, among others, as it offers training for beginning genealogists.[88])

Persons descended from Sambuca's emigrants are almost certainly also using *Ancestry.com*'s DNA search capacity but their numbers are impossible to estimate. Appearing in my Google Website searches is one report—again from Rockford, Illinois—that reports on surprising results from a DNA search by a man who believed he was of Swedish origin. (Swedes were among the earliest immigrants to Rockford, where they dominated the town's furniture industry.[89]) Rockford resident Dick Nelson recalled feeling since childhood that he was different from the rest of his family--in part because of his dark coloration and in part because of the unusual educational path he chose. (In a family of high-school dropouts, he eventually became a college professor.) Nelson's *Ancestry.com* DNA confirmed a preponderance of Italian/Greek DNA and almost no Swedish ancestry. Initially upset, he began to question elderly family members who eventually revealed that his father was a Sicilian; whether the man had had an affair with Nelson's paternal aunt or with his (deceased) mother is not clear from the narrative. According to Nelson, the Sicilian was a well-known "Rockford figure and upstanding citizen who served as Democratic committeeman and deputy sheriff" in the town. Pursing genealogical information about his father's family, Nelson traveled to Sambuca; his paternal grandfather's birth certificate appeared on the Webpage with his interview.[90] (His peasant father also appears in my pre-digital compilation of migrants from the town.)

Despite its vast size, *Ancestry.com* does not completely dominate the Google Search Analytics summarized in Table 1. Instead its digital archive of Webpages points to sizeable community of

---

[88] https://www.ancestry.com/academy/courses/recommended. Accessed April 29, 2018.
[89] See "A Look Back....The Story of Rockford Furniture," *The Rock River Times*, January 1, 2015, http://rockrivertimes.com/2015/01/01/a-look-backthe-story-of-rockford-furniture/. Accessed April 29, 2018.
[90] Sarah Wolf, "Rockford Native Left in 'Total Shock' after Receiving Ancestry.com DNA Results," *Rockford Register Star*, December 2, 2016.

Sambuca-origin genealogists participating in an array of genealogy Websites that flourished before the expansion of *Ancestry.com* in the first years of twenty-first century, around the time I also received my first and only query from Sambuca-origin family historian, Nick Gagliano. At the heart of this community was a small group of largely midwestern female genealogists descended, like Rosalia Abbate's great-grandson, from the peasants who had first traveled from Sambuca to New Orleans before moving along the railroad lines (that employed many of them) to cities like Baton Rouge, Kansas City, Chicago and Rockford and to farming communities in Louisiana and Texas and smaller mining and industrial sites In Illinois, Wisconsin, Iowa and Indiana.[91] The Sambuca-origin genealogists exhibited a growing distrust of *Ancestry.com* as it transformed digital archives into generators of profit.

In the late 1990s and early 2000s Sambuca-origin genealogists and family historians posted information and queries on RootsWeb (and the related WorldGenWeb), *Genealogy.com, ItalianGenealogy.com,* Wikitree, World Vital Records, MyHeritage and others.[92] Although I cannot know if the researchers used them, Websites offering to conduct genealogical research for persons with roots in Sambuca (and almost every other Italian town) began to appear somewhat later.[93] Of the many available options, RootsWeb became the preferred site for digital communication among Sambuca-origin genealogists; as the group consolidated it confronted changing *An-*

---

[91] I explore this group in some detail in a paper titled "Sambuca's Genealogists," Migranti di Sicilia. I quaderni del Museo dell'emigrazione 14 (2018).

[92] As more than one genealogist has pointed out, "Trying to compare the holdings of the different subscription sites is one of the most frustrating parts of 'doing genealogy'. Trying to determine the differences between the regular consumer version of the websites and their library editions is also difficult." https://genealogy.stackexchange.com/questions/10545/whats-the-difference-between-the-world-vital-records-and-my-heritage-databases?utm_medium=organic&utm_source=google_rich_qa&utm_campaign=google_rich_qa. Accessed April 29, 2018. Whatever its limitations (including the significant subscription fees it charges), one must concede that in this respect *Ancestry.com* has simplified access to genealogical materials.

[93] See http://www.italianside.com/sicilia/agrigento/sambuca-di-sicilia/; https://www.gentracer.com/sambucadisicilia.html. Accessed April 28, 2018.

cestry.com policies and eventually created the independent "Club Sambuca" website.

RootsWeb began in 2003 as the "Roots Surname List." According to a Wikipedia entry RootsWeb was free; its purpose was to help people research their family histories. It facilitated the uploading of GEDCOM files (generated by the extremely popular digital tool FamilyTreeMaker) and the sharing of family trees created with that tool. From April 2004 until June 2015, descendants of Sambuca's migrants rather intensively engaged with each on a RootsWeb online forum formally named ITA-SAMBUCA-DI-SICILIA. Over a decade, almost 2,000 messages were posted and circulated by 300 different correspondents.

Welcoming researchers to ITA-SAMBUCA-DI-SICILIA/) in May 2004, was a woman from the American Midwest named MC.[94] MC became the leading voice of ITA-SAMBUCA-DI-SICILIA/ and remained in that role for over a decade. The group's discussions were wide-ranging and provide a good introduction not only to the motivations of citizen researcher genealogists but also to their research practices, which included a desire for freely cooperating and open sharing of many kinds of information, not just genealogical matters.

Sambuca-origin genealogists regularly shared their motivations for "roots-seeking" through research. Many who listed the cluster of surnames they were researching signalled their hope of identifying and finding kin who had been lost during migration to and life in the United States. Wrote DQ, on March 10, 2007, "I just know all of us [sharing a surname] must be related in one way or another these names show up in so many places and we know that back then they had big familys that went all over America and beyond. Anyway I know we care for each other even though we are or maybe not related." Many novices also shared their disappointment when they quickly realized that "half the town were

---

[94] Since I have not sought permission to use personal names from individual members of these groups, I have chosen to use initials (representing pseudonyms) for individuals authoring messages.

Cacioppo's."[95] The most frustrated new genealogists simply gave up and quickly withdrew from communication. But others were rewarded and found relatives (usually called "cousins") in both the United States and Sambuca. One woman reported writing to every person sharing her grandfather's last name in the Sambuca telephone book before connecting with one who spoke English. (She later described their visit in Sambuca at great length.) Another shared with the entire listserv his response to the genealogist who had assisted him in searching for family members in online sources, noting "My Mother Maria Audienz [sic] is 86, and sister Carmella is 83 and they remember your grandfather very well."[96]

In 2006-2007, correspondents on ITA-SAMBUCA-DI-SICILIA discussed another motivation to pursue genealogical research. Many had parents and grandparents who had vigorously rebuffed their early efforts to know more about their family's past. As "SA" wrote in April 2007, "What was going on that they didn't want us to know?" Tales of family silences and "stone walling" poured forth in response to her question; apparently many others had puzzled over their relatives' reluctance to talk about the past. AD sympathized with SA, noting "When I started asking simple questions I was told by my Great Aunt that I had better leave it alone and that was that. I have chosen to continue my search, but it will be with out help from them. I don't want to hurt anyone nor do I want to rekindle old feelings that have been buried." Another correspondent, AK, assumed that silence protected ugly secrets, "There is so many things our people held in secret because we always keep our 'dirty laundry to ourselves,' (grandmother's famous words.)" GT was one of many to suggest that family silences sought to hide criminality, for example involvement with the Black Hand or the Mafia. (GT later also notified the listserv he had written a novel about a Sicilian criminal, presumably from his

---

[95] SA, message dated April 8, 2007.
[96] Message from FG, January 2, 2006.

family.[97]) NA reported finding the same problem in Sicily, where "One of my cousins who lives in Cefalù Sicily will not give me any information on my paternal side of the family, because as he puts it, 'the past should remain in the past.' That was all he had to say, now I am looking harder than ever."[98]

Even when Sambuca-origin genealogists failed to find cousins or fill their family's silences with new stories, they often succeeded in forming satisfying relationships by sharing news and research advice. ITA-SAMBUCA-DI-SICILIA fostered friendship and a kind of casual intimacy. Overall, communication was civil and supportive; conflicts when they occurred were confronted quickly and did not long disrupt the group. Intermittently, the most active members of the group lavished praise on each other. Understandably, the moderator, "MC," received the largest encomiums. On March 2, 2006, VG let the entire group know of the research assistance MC had provided and praised her "unselfish dedication" to a search for a missing cousin. She reported "I have been able to have a telephone conversation with 93 years old 'MM' (daughter of my grandmother's lost brother"). Another responded, "You won't get any argument from me...I think [MC is] an amazing lady and that we are very fortunate to have her as our Web Mother!" Some imagined the Sambuca origin genealogists as a largely loving and supportive family that shared generously knowledge, skills, and contacts (or, as they usually described them, "connections"). Over the years, moderator MC repeatedly assisted other genealogists in what she called "look-ups" in collections of Sambuca birth records made available through local libraries by LDS (Latter Day Saints). Another correspondent who signed her message with "Hugs," offered to find grave sites in a

---

[97] It can still be purchased on Amazon.com, Tony Racina (a pen name), *Trinacria: When Life Begins, Death is Born* (Charleston, SC: CreateSpace, 2010). CreateSpace facilitates self-publishing and distribution through Amazon. The acknowledged criminal in the family as a motivator of family history research is also a key theme in Helene Stupinski's *Murder in Matera, A True Story of Passion, Family, and Forgiveness in Southern Italy* (New York: Dey Street/William Morrow, 2017).
[98] Message from AG, July 11, 2009.

Louisiana cemetery where she went annually to place flowers on her father's grave. Sharing Italian language skills fostered other relationships, VG, who lived in London but returned to Sambuca each summer circulated her phone numbers so listserv participants could consult while visiting Sicily.

In fact, heritage tourism and the sharing of information about travel to Sambuca became an important focus of ITA-SAMBUCA-DI-SICILIA during its middle years, especially in the spring and summer months. Many shared stories of travels to the town and their impressions of it, commenting on the beauty of the countryside or the town's location. Surprisingly few visits to the town were motivated by the desire to pursue further genealogical research; most who visited Sambuca described themselves as visiting tourist sites and seeking emotional re-connections with ancestors, living kin or the local landscape (which MC called "the lay of the land.") Returned genealogists also told funny and self-deprecating stories about their experiences as Americans driving a car with standard transmission or misunderstanding directions or local customs. In 2007 a small controversy broke out among visitors who found Sicily's accommodations modern and up-to-date—just like in America, some insisted --and those who had less positive experiences or did not want to replicate the familiar experiences and hotels known from their tourism in the United States. Wrote one, "If it's just like Kansas, why go?" Names and directions to inns and *agriturismo* sites were also frequently shared.[99]

ITA-SAMBUCA-DI-SICILIA began to change in 2008, when RootsWeb was purchased by MyFamily.com, a commercial network of family history sites that included *Ancestry.com*. RootsWeb users expressed a wide array of opinions about the change—some feared they could not afford the fees for access that were sure to come, while others seemed concerned that shadowy but powerful internet corporations would monetize their family data. The

---

[99] For a particularly rich, early description of a visit see the message from BM, October 24, 2004.

thought angered many.[100] Although subscribers to ITA-SAMBUCA-DI-SICILIA did not comment extensively on the purchase of RootsWeb, communication on the listserv fell sharply after 2008 and never again bounced back to levels attained two years earlier. The sale apparently challenged many genealogists' implicit commitments to open sharing and many who had participated in ITA-SAMBUCA-DI-SICILIA sought new ways to shared information and keep it free, for example by transcribing information from ships manifests for any migrant who had given Sambuca as their previous residence. Moderator MC also began to create an index of names from digitized versions of Sambuca's birth records after 1873. Somewhat later, someone transcribed American military records of men listing their birth in Sambuca. When *Ancestry.com* stopped supporting Family Tree Maker files in 2015, communication on ITA-SAMBUCA-DI-SICILIA effectively ceased, and communication and sharing began to shift to a new, independent Website.[101]

Already in 2004, MC had announced on the ITA-SAMBUCA-DI-SICILIA listserv that she had created an *Aol.com* site, "Sambuca Club." According to MC, her Chicago immigrant grandparents had told her that the Sambucesi of that city "would get together for dinners and companionship. They called this group called themselves [sic] 'The Sambuca Club.'"[102] The historical Sambuca Club was one of thousands of immigrant clubs, with historical

---

[100] "Opinions on the MyFamily-RootsWeb Merger," *Family Tree Magazine*, August 20, 2008. https://www.familytreemagazine.com/premium/2000-merger-poll/. For a description of how RootsWeb data was being upscaled, see the description of the WorldConnect project, which was initiated by RootsWeb in the mid1990s: https://wc.RootsWeb.ancestry.com/wchistory.html.

[101] In January 2018 the "RootsWeb Team" reported that a security breach had caused it to take almost all listserv content (along with the content of most other RootsWeb listservs or "message boards") offline. https://web.archive.org/web/20150909230526/http://archiver.RootsWeb.ancestry.com/th/index/ITA-SAMBUCA-DI-SICILIA/).

[102] See the announcement of the Sambuca Club website, ITA-SAMBUCA-DI-SICILIA index, November, 2004: https://web.archive.org/web/20151023201402/http://archiver.RootsWeb.ancestry.com/th/index/ITA-SAMBUCA-DI-SICILIA/2004-11.

roots in the *circoli* and mutual aid societies that had flourished in late nineteenth-century Sicily. In April 2009, soon after the sale of RootsWeb and the controversy on RootsWeb over looming commercialization, listserv moderator MC notified all subscribers that the leaders of the Vigo Lodge, Order of Sons of Italy of Rockford Illinois had purchased the domain name www.SambucaClub.org.[103] The Lodge's leaders asked the group to "please accept this as token of our appreciation for all of your efforts for preserving our Italian culture and heritage." MC herself added, "This new link will make it much easier for everyone to find and remember us.... It is much easier to put spreadsheets and things on the web site now. If you have anything that you would like to contribute, I can easily upload them to the site."

Today, a bilingual description of the Club notes "The Sambuca Club is a group of researchers dedicated to finding their ancestors of Sambuca." A separate section, created on the request of longtime Sambuca supporters and translator Giuseppe Cacioppo offers (in Italian) assistance to people living in Sambuca who hope to contact relatives in the United States. For lovers of Sambuca the drink, the site also warns "This is for Sambuca di Sicilia ONLY!" The site's home page includes the town's crest, in color, photos from the countryside around Sambuca, and an invitation to attend a meeting, the annual dinner dance or the annual St. Joseph's Table organized by a group called "The St. Mary's of Sambuca of Chicago." On the left side of the page, links take the visitor to photo collections documenting individual families and their visits to Sambuca, the annual festival held in Rockford, Illinois, and varied historical documentation (including the story written by Rosalia Abbate's great grandson) compiled in Rockford. The right side of the page features links leading to more photographs and reminiscences, an article about the genealogists that appeared *La Voce di Sambuca*, the emails of about 50 members of the Sambuca Club, and the indices of births recorded for Sambuca 1873-1899 (along with instructions for ordering copies), ships manifests information and draft records

---

[103] Message from "MC" dated April 19, 2009.

described above. There are also historical documents describing Sambucesi's campaign to support Sambuca's Orphanage, and information for those planning to visit Sambuca. Just as moderator MC had shaped the dialogue on ITA-SAMBUCA-DI-SICILIA for a decade, her influence on www.SambucaClub.org remains very visible. MC makes her intentions and good will as clear as she can by stating in both languages, "This is a labor of love. I welcome any and all who wish to further their research of Sambuca." It is unclear how much traffic Club Sambuca attracts but when the family historian and retired lawyer Nick Gagliano urged me to update my pre-digital research on 3500 emigrants from Sambuca in digital formats so others could use it, "Club Sambuca" provided the best evidence I could find that Nick was not the only citizen researcher interested and already knowledgeable about a town I had not researched further since the 1980s.

Bridging the chasm between citizen researchers and professional historians Nick Gagliano wrote me an email in early summer, 2016, 15 years after I had mailed to him 71 pounds of paper transcribing the records I had examined in Sambuca's archive in the 1970s and 1980s. In 2001, Nick had hoped to create an Italian American historical museum and he had hoped further it could transform those 71 pounds of paper into a database accessible to genealogists and family historians visiting the museum. When Nick reappeared in 2016, he assured me my research had not washed away during Hurricane Katrina but had to admit the museum simply did not have the resources to create the database he had envisioned. Nick begged me to take back my research files and to find a student assistant to create the database. By 2016, furthermore, Nick had still higher hopes--that the database itself be posted online, finding the largest possible audience. Having located his own father in my research files, and to express his gratitude (or perhaps merely to spur me on), he then sent me a copy of the history of his family that he had written. It was over fifty single-spaced pages — a rich, carefully researched and very detailed family history.

Revisiting those pounds of paper, I quickly realized that no student I could afford to pay would possess sufficient knowledge of Sambuca to interpret my handwritten transcriptions from documents in rural Sicily so I decided to do the work myself. During the first four months of 2017, the day-long bouts of extremely dull, routine labor that I put into data entry left me with plenty of time to think about any new questions to be asked or old questions to be revisited. I recognized that with a relational digital database I could both map the neighborhood locations of Sambucesi in Sambuca and across the United States and use digital tools to more quickly and systematically analyze extended kinship networks among migrants. The digital revolution made it possible for the first time to resolve one of the largest unanswered questions of my pre-digital resource, which had been to measure the relative importance of neighborhood friendships and kinship in the choice of destination in United States. I also had plenty of time to ponder how a database that drew mainly on Sambuca's archives might now be expanded and extended through exploration and entry of the American documents and public family trees so easily searchable through *Ancestry.com*. When bored with data entry, furthermore, I soon began my search for other digital information about Sambuca. Once I discovered "Sambuca Club" I began to wonder if the information compiled there — the family trees, photos, family histories, and transcribed lists of ships manifest and draft records might be integrated into a database and whether genealogists might even contribute to "crowdsourcing" the entry of American information in the database as they researched their own families.[104] I began searching *Ancestry.com* for some of the 3500 emigrants in my new relational database; the work was also tedious but it greatly enriched many of the rather bare human descriptions from Sambuca's archives.

---

[104] For a definition of crowdsourcing, see Geoffrey Rockwell, "Crowdsourcing the Humanities," in *Collaborative Research in the Digital Humanities*, ed. Marilyn Deegan and Willard McCarty (Farnham, Surrey: Ashgate, 2012), pp. 135-54.

Remembering Nick's courage in reaching out to me in 2001, I summoned up the courage in late November 2017 to write to MC and introduce myself. I wrote to Nick at the same time to tell him of the progress that had been made toward fulfilling his dream. But I never received a reply.[105]

CONCLUSION

To date, the digital revolution has had a far more profound impact outside the scholarly world than within it. By comparing the research practices and questions of the 1970s to practices and questions created or transformed by the digital revolution, this paper has presented a detailed examination of its impact both in and outside the scholarly world. My exploration of the significance of digital tools, methods, and archives aimed to identify changes that have proved relevant and even welcome for researchers. Ultimately, however, I suggest that any twenty-first century scholar who approaches the digital archive with the same questions about Sambuca di Sicilia that motivated most research in the 1970s and 1980s would produce answers that differ only modestly from earlier ones. Research in digital archives can extend analyses of culture and political economy beyond the peasant past into the commercialization of folklore, the past and "heritage" as incentives to tourism in the twenty-first century. And the ready (if gated) access to the vast and expanding digital archive compiled as *Ancestry.com*, along with new digital tools for mapping and network analysis, might allow revised and more detailed and nuanced answers to questions about the structure of migrants' migration chains (and especially the relative importance of neighborly and kinship ties in creating "links") and the transnational occupational and class mobility patterns of

---

[105] I dedicate this paper to Nicholas Gagliano who died at age 92 in March, 2018. Nick was truly a visionary who understood the scholarly promise of the digital revolution much earlier than I did. I wish Nick could have lived to encourage and participate in a renewed joint effort to bridge the chasm that usually separated citizen and professional researchers. See http://www.legacy.com/guestbooks/nola/nicholas-joseph-gagliano-condolences/188588417?&nocache=true&cid=addentry&sign=0 Accessed April 29, 2018.

Sambuca's peasant and artisan emigrants across several generations.

The circle of scholars who remain interested in the questions of the 1970s and 1980s has dwindled, even as the numbers of citizen researchers and genealogists interested in rural southern Italy have grown exponentially. The revolutionary potential of the digital revolution for scholars has been to facilitate the posing of new questions—especially about contemporary political economy and culture--rather than the creating the likelihood of generating new answers to old questions. This scholarly dynamic of seeking new questions is itself nothing new and cannot be attributed exclusively to the digital revolution. Since at least the second half of the twentieth century, if not for much longer, questions of an older scholarly generation often fail to animate or excite the rising scholarly generation. On the contrary, the apprentice-like training of new scholars encourages each scholarly generation to differentiate its own work from that of its own mentors by posing new questions and using new archives. At the very most each new generation of scholars views itself as building "on" but also "beyond" the work of their elders and mentors. Especially in scholarship on rural southern Italy and the region's migrants to the Americas, it was not the digital revolution that drove the shift from social historical studies emphasizing structure and structural change and alteration in human life toward cultural studies focused instead on human subjectivity, representation and meaning. In any case, cultural studies scholars to date have not yet made extensive use of the kinds of digital archives this paper documents.

The impact of the digital revolution has been much greater for citizen researchers, and especially for genealogists. Once the domain of elites with time and money to travel to scattered archives, genealogy in recent years has been democratized and integrated by the descendants of working-class southern and eastern European and Asian immigrants to the United States. The digital revolution has facilitated research and communication among the growing numbers of Americans descended from residents of rural towns like Sambuca di Sicilia as they began to search for a "return" to their "roots" in the 1970s. The scholarly questions of the 1970s and 1980s have also rather belatedly inspired professional historians such as me to turn to the same digital archives that have facilitated the democratization of genealogy. Transatlantic record linkage is now possible and even easy but communication between citizen researchers and professional scholars using the same digital archives remains fraught, and highly unusual.

Nevertheless, a final, significant consequence of the digital revolution has been the increased ease with which genealogists and professional historians could, if they wish to do so, identify and communicate with each other. I became aware of this possibility already in the 1990s when I saw how email increased the numbers of persons who had read *From Sicily to Elizabeth Street* and took the initiative to contact me, either to share family stories or to ask whether I had any information about their relatives. But it was the Louisiana-based family historian and retired lawyer, descended from a peasant family in Sambuca, Nick Gagliano who first contacted me with idea that the migrant data I had compiled in the 1970s might be digitized and made available to citizen researchers like him. It took almost 20 years for the two of us to see a way forward. If the two groups of researchers can communicate, then they can also, potentially at least, collaborate. Digitizing the information on 3,500 emigrated Sambucesi that I collected forty years ago in Sambuca's archive encouraged me first to learn about and then, finally, to reach out to genealogists who had long been working in the digital archive as citizen researchers.

Whether or not I can as a professional historian find a way to cooperate and share with the network of genealogists descended from Sambuca's migrants remains an open question. It is not at all obvious that the kind of family trees created by scores of genealogists can be harmonized with the kind of relational database I have created from evidence transcribed in the 1970s and 1980s in Sambuca's archive. Professional historians and genealogists continue to be motivated by very different passions; they mine *Ancestry.com* and compile its data for vastly different purposes and in vastly different forms. Only by attempting to harmonize the fruits of the considerable research labor of both groups will it become obvious, over time, whether the desires of either or both can be met through collaboration.

The Orphanage
Encounters in Transnational Space

ROBERT VISCUSI

THINGS WE NEVER TALK ABOUT BUT NEVER FORGET

Relations between Italians and Italian Americans are often uncomfortable. Italians find Italian Americans embarrassing—ill-bred *cafoni* with country manners and loud voices. The *arriviste* who returns to Italy in the guise of a free-spending braggart who puts his relatives to shame has a name in Italian: the American uncle (*lo zio d'America*). Italian Americans find Italians equally embarrassing, though for different reasons: Italians are too dressy and too lofty by half. Their politics appear both incomprehensible and unrespectable. Think Silvio Berlusconi. Italy's behavior in the Second World War inspired neither trust nor admiration. Think Benito Mussolini.

What lies under this mutual distaste? For many Italians and Italian Americans, this relationship retains the bitterest flavor of sibling rivalry, a condition where mutual distrust, envy, spite, and name-calling are endemic. I suggest that we isolate from other transnational spaces the one that Italians and Italian Americans share. This space has a specific character. It is an orphanage.

WHAT YOU SEE AND WHAT YOU DON'T

The Columbus Day Parade, as celebrated in New York City, is a triumphal march where Italian Americans display the trophies of their victories alongside trophies of Italian commerce. There are marching bands playing familiar anthems. There is an abundance of energetic youths, displaying the fecundity and flowering of the tribe, cavorting on floats that represent the caravels of Columbus; there are strings of Ferraris and Lamborghinis, reminding everyone of Italian mastery in international trade; there are politicians (themselves a show of force); there are Sicilian painted donkey carts where scantily dressed young lovers toast one another with imported wines; there are dancers and singers and movie stars. This spectacle of Italian America, as florid as a pizza and almost as familiar, celebrates a show of abundance. Not especially a comprehensive portrayal. Carnival, not Lent. Far more expressive of the soul of Italian Americans—of their emotional and affective truth—is the procession when they carry the statue of the saint through the streets, praying for help like orphans crying out for their mothers.[1] Between Italy and Italian America there lies a wide void where suffering and uncertainty have made themselves known and felt throughout the history of this transnational space, which I believe changed its shape after Italy signed the Maastricht Treaty in 1993.

In this essay, I have painted in miniature the internal dynamics of the relations between Italians in Italy and Italians in the United States of America during the long twentieth century—roughly 1891 to 1993—when Italians went everywhere, to be sure, but discovered a distinct destiny in the United States as it became the megalith of the contemporary world. My privileged witnesses are memoirists and novelists and essayists and poets, those who concern themselves with the geography of the inner world.

FROM ITALY TO TRANSNATIONAL SPACE

Italy may or may not be a failed state, but it is certainly a failed revolution. The Risorgimento (1821-1861) promised a great deal to Italy's poor and excluded populations. It expressed their emotions in its ideology. Indeed, it stood on a long history that joined the sorrows of the poor with the frustrations of well-to-do Italians:

> Noi fummo da secoli
> Calpesti, derisi,
> Perché non siam popolo,
> Perche siam divisi.
>
> [We were for centuries
> Trampled, scorned,

---

[1] There are fewer and fewer of these processions nowadays. Their emotional accuracy still strikes a recognizable chord. The classic version is portrayed in Robert Orsi, *The Madonna of 115th Street* (New Haven: Yale University Press, 1985).

Because we weren't a people.
Because we were divided.][2]

Rich or poor, whoever sang this war anthem recognized its thumbnail sketch of post-Imperial Italian failures. These failures inspired the diplomats, soldiers, and guerrillas who populated the nineteenth-century insurrection that aimed to produce a nation. The military and diplomatic successes of the Risorgimento were at best implausible. To be sure, when seen against the long background of ignominy that preceded them, these victories now seem almost uncanny. The Risorgimento raised great hopes, but these were destined to go largely unfulfilled. Indeed, United Italy, whether as a kingdom (1861-1947) or as a republic (1948-present), has yet to conduct its civil and political affairs with a level of distinction (whether real or imagined) remotely comparable with the brilliance of its war of unification. During its first fifty years of existence, the Regno proved itself unable to fulfill its promise to the poor of Italy, who left in droves, depopulating whole provinces in the search of a more generous destiny—in the Americas south and north, in Italy's doomed African colonies, in Scotland and Switzerland, France and Belgium and Germany.

There are many ways to think of where they were going. Yes, they were definitely leaving Italy, entering a large variety of national and subnational cultures, climates and microclimates of invention and habitation. But many were not really leaving at all. Italian Americans, in particular, were entering instead a large transnational and transactional space, full of destinations and crosshatched with vectors, where many of them would continue to work directly with Italy as a nation, a partner, and a metropole.

Relations between Italians inside Italy and Italians outside of it are a large subject that can be approached in many ways. Migration historians tell us that 50% of the Italians who left during the years of the Great Migration (1880-1924) returned to Italy at least once, some-

---

[2] Goffredo Mameli, "Il Canto degli italiani" (All translations mine).

times more than once. While the Fascist regime and the Second World War sharply interrupted this rhythm of return, the liberalization of U.S. immigration quotas in the 1950s primed the pump from Italy with relatively well educated migrants, and the economic progress of Italians outside Italy enabled them to engage in a new level of reconnection with the roots of their national culture and the branches of their families, towns, and provinces in the *madrepatria*. That their social ambitions should involve renewed involvement with a nation they had abandoned calls for some comment.

It is clear that most Italian emigrants did not choose to settle in the United States, but went instead to many other countries in the Americas and in Europe. These settlers soon enough lost their sense of belonging to Italy with any sort of anagraphic filiation. They came to identify themselves as Argentines, Brazilians, Germans, and Swiss without the need of the prefix *Italian*, let alone a hyphen to bundle two identities together. In the United States, this adoption of a new identity did not always so cleanly take place. Donna Gabaccia's explanation of what happened instead is enlightening. She underlines that "the United States shares with Canada and Australia a long history of subjecting and conquering the indigenous peoples it conquered." She adds the following:

> France, Canada, Germany, Australia, and Argentina are just as much nations of immigrants as the United States is, yet none has generated an equivalent of the immigrant paradigm as symbol of their nation's distinctiveness.
>
> [...]
>
> Histories of Argentina, Brazil, and France show limited interest in migrants once they have become citizens and entered the nation.
>
> [...]
>
> What makes the United States different from Canada and Australia is its long history of slavery as a source of significant national disunity. It is this history ... that explains the creation of

immigrant paradigm in the United States and not in other English-speaking countries.[3]

In the United States, the Italians came to occupy an ethnic silo homologous with, and often physically adjacent to, the one to which African Americans were consigned. Their condition was not quite the social death of slaves, but it was hardly that of the American citizen freely enjoying the rights to life, liberty, and the pursuit of happiness. Immigrants who settled in the United States who remained attached to a national identity they had supposedly left behind were marking themselves and their posterity with the signs of their civil disabilities and their abject condition. The complexity of their situation stands forth in the sequence of events surrounding the lynching of eleven Sicilian immigrants in New Orleans in 1891. Clearly, the Sicilians were despised much as the African Americans who lived in the same neighborhoods. The lynching followed the pattern of African American lynchings, with approval at the highest level. In this case, the mayor, one Joseph Shakespeare, was the responsible party. President McKinley was unmoved by claims that the federal government should indemnify the families of the lynched Sicilians. For justice the Sicilians had to appeal to the Italian government, which placed an embargo on exports of American pork until such time as the United States paid the indemnity. This narrative provided a template that was roughly followed ever afterwards. Italian immigrants secured their civil rights in the United States with the term *Italian-American*, which tied them together with their co-nationals on the other side of the ocean.

TRANSNATIONAL SPACE

That solution has only worked at the price of locating Italian Americans (*qua* Italian Americans) firmly in transnational space, not entirely here and not entirely there. Transnational space is both

---

[3] Donna Gabaccia, "Is Everywhere Nowhere? Nomads, Nations, and the Immigrant Paradigm of United States History," *Journal of American History* 86.3 (1999): 1132, 1133.

full and empty. On the one hand, it is thick with commerce: oils and silks and manufactures of every kind, wines and children and priests and women; paintings and sculptures and richly-wrought caskets filled with treasures. On the other hand, transnational space is a void. It is that aspect of national space where no one, in fact, belongs. It is, clearly, an aspect of the national system. Before there were nations, the ocean and the sky belonged to the gods. But afterwards they became wastes, where no one had roots or parents.

The twentieth century, with its vast multitudes in flight from improvident regimes and malignant states, has become a chronotope where the transnational void afflicts not only those who are driven out of their homes but also, by a well known reflexive mechanism of self-awareness, it afflicts those who initiate, and even those who passively witness, the driving out of others. The encounter of those who stay with those who go is so persistent, so ubiquitous, that it renders transnational space a site where dispossession is sometimes universal. I say *sometimes* because we are speaking of a way of seeing, a way of feeling that underlies other dynamic emotions. How large is this *regno doloroso* remains to be seen.

Transnational space is a void, where many things have been removed that can never actually be replaced. When Italian Americans consider Italy, they are working with a drastically reduced encyclopedia. They may know the name of the town, let us say, but do they know who lives there any more? Do they still speak the dialect? Do they speak the standard dialect, or even a regional variety, of Italian? Do they know the names of the merchants in the town? What ideas do they have of the political life of the town, the region, the province, the nation? Do they know the names and programs of the political factions? On the other side of the map, the Italians are working with an equally inadequate toolkit. Do they know even the names of any relatives or friends in the United States? Where do they get their ideas of American local, state, regional, national, or international concerns and policies? These are just a few of the things that are often missing. On the one side, when people leave a place they have known intimately, they will miss it on the most intimate levels of cognition. All of the senses will feel the lack: the garlic has a different taste, the air another perfume, the weather has new rhythms of change, the trees and the flowers and the heights of the hills, the colors of the skies and mountains are all strangers. On the other side, if one does not know the language of the new place, one slips into a tiny world of discourse. If one learns the language, the process has many levels of mastery. Daily life, in the rites of food and love and work and rent, presents the most isolating lessons in language, either sending the migrant back to the familiar words of the mother tongue, or narrowing the focus of discourse in the new language. In one's native place, wider concerns—legal, narrative, interpersonal, theoretical, theological—more readily come to the tongue, and thus, to the mind.

Images cross the ocean in drastically reduced forms and give way to lurid distortions. Popular ideologies deal in schematic notions and industrialized nostalgia. The transatlantic space is intellectually thin, but emotionally it is a force field of considerable intensity. Its gravitational pull arises from unfathomable depths of political culture, where institutional, legal, and ideological histories mingle and breed continuously, always producing new forms with deep ties to their predecessors. At the bottom of the transatlantic space, there is a seam from which emerges a steady flow of indelible stereotypes.

We have a metaphor to explore, outlining some ways that Italian and Italian American writers have dealt with the ideological force fields of the transnational space they share. A complete survey of so complex a terrain is impossible, but I will focus on the peculiar history that attaches to the orphanage, which amounts to a figure for this particular transnational situation. In the orphanage, the winds that blow speak of the remembered or dismembered world of the past, or they tell of the possible or impossible world of the future. The local world, the present time, of the orphanage is more than anything else the crossing place of ideological programs which may, and indeed do, arise from every quadrant of the chart.

THE RAISED FIST

Edmondo De Amicis (1846-1908) describes the departure of emigrants on a steamship leaving Genoa for Buenos Aires. They have been loaded into the steerage they will share with livestock and every other sort of cargo, and now they turn to face the city they are leaving:

> The city already glowed with lights. The steamer glided silently through the half-darkness of the port, almost furtively, as if it carried away a cargo of stolen human flesh. I pushed myself towards the bow, into the thick of the crowd, which was all turned towards the land, to watch the amphitheater of Genoa, which was now rapidly lighting up. A few of them spoke in a low voice. Here and there in the dark, I could make out seated women, babies at the breast, with their heads in their hands. Near the forecastle, a rough and solitary voice cried out in sarcastic tones—"Viva L'Italia!"—and lifting my gaze, I saw a tall old man who raised his fist to the fatherland. When we left were beyond the port, it was night.[4]

De Amicis the observant nationalist takes ship with a load of immigrants and sails with them all the way to Buenos Aires, providing a brilliant account of life in steerage—seen, as it were, from above—for his bourgeois readers. The passage above is a supreme sample drawn from the large archive left behind by journalists and novelists with good educations going among the *terroni* and *emigrati* and reporting back to their metropolitan readers in the pages of newspapers and travel books: Dario Papa, Adolfo Rossi, Ferdinando Fontana. They were anthropologists in everything—in class, in sympathy for the oppressed, in prose style—in everything, that is, except method. Unlike the cagey social scientists of those days, these writers included in their kits the arts of dramatizing their own positions, of rendering scenic and even comic the

---

[4] Edmondo De Amicis, *Sull'Oceano*, Introduction by Franco Custodi (Milan: Garzanti, 1996 [1889]) 8.

differences between themselves and the people whose hopes and sorrows they were observing. They were not so much dispassionate observers as they were *simpatici* among friends, cabin-class passengers sharing their observations with their companions in the lounge.

The old man with his fist in the air spoke for the mass of poor emigrants, whose disappointment with Italy would not leave them for a long time. There were many such among the Italians in the United States. They became socialists, communists, union organizers, anarchists. Gaetano Bresci (1869-1901), a silk weaver from Coiano near Prato in Tuscany, migrated to the United States in 1896, fresh from imprisonment on the island of Lampedusa for his anarchist activities. By 1898, he was married and living in Paterson, New Jersey, where he found work in his craft and companions in his struggle for justice and equality among the anarchist silk workers of that town. That same year, events in Milan posed a definitive challenge to him. Bread prices rose, leading to mass protests. King Umberto ordered General Bava-Beccaris to put down the strike, and the officer responded by having his soldiers open fire on the protesters with rifles and cannon. At least four hundred people were hit, and at least ninety of them died outright, including the sister of Gaetano Bresci. Some might have expected the king to reprimand the general for his excess. But Umberto was grateful to the general for defending the royal family, and awarded him the highest military honors. Bresci, like radicals around the world, was outraged. Telling no one of his plan, he went back to Milan. On the night of July 29, 1900, near the royal villa in Monza, he shot the king three times in the head, killing him instantly. Bresci was immediately apprehended, and was soon tried and found guilty. "I did not shoot the king. I shot a principle," was his defense. Among the many who condemned him for his act of summary justice was Edmondo De Amicis, whose sympathies, while broad, not surprisingly did not embrace terrorists. There was no capital punishment in Milan, so Bresci was sentenced to life in prison, where there was no sympathy awaiting him, either. The following year he was found hung in his cell. He became a martyr of anarchism and the first Italian American to intervene decisively in the history of the country he had left.

THE PICK AND SHOVEL POET AND THE MISSIONARY'S WIFE

Many voyages become acts of vengeance. They inflict unforgivable losses whose memory colors the transnational space that Italians and Italian Americans share in markedly different modes. It may seem that Italian Americans make more of these memories, the ocean with its size and its sorrows rolling on in the background of many of their twentieth century recollections. Many of these migrants, living as well as dead, wash up on the shores of New York and New Jersey—and they are alone, their families having been left behind or, just as frequently, splintered while trying to gain a foothold on the steeps of American livelihood. Pascal D'Angelo, the "pick and shovel poet" in his memoir *Son of Italy* writes of struggling to make his way as a laborer in the United States alongside his father. The two have come to America together with others from the pastoral poverty of Introdacqua in Abruzzo. His father eventually gives up the struggle and returns to Introdacqua, but Pascal makes his way, partly in the company of fellow laborers and largely all alone in the public libraries—and at a fateful performance of *Aida* he attends one summer evening at the Sheepshead Bay Racetrack. His is the perfect orphanage life recounted by many Horatio Alger types in immigrant literature— shoeshine boys, farmhands, hobos, street-corner philosophers. This displaced shepherd's discovery of *Aida* is a belated encounter with his Italian national identity. This meeting makes him a poet, according to his own accounting of its effect upon him. It does not heal the breach or answer the aloneness.

Nor is this aloneness a curse that afflicts only the poor immigrant. In the 1920s, the distinguished Italian journalist Luigi Barzini, Sr., moved with his family to New York, where he founded and directed the *Corriere d'America* from 1922 to 1931. In the memoir of his son, the even more distinguished Luigi Barzini, Jr., the sorrows and frustrations of well-bred Italians in the United States get full attention. In a *tour-de-force* of understatement, he describes his mother's difficulties with American life:

> For some reason, she never felt happy in the United States. She had few friends and it was difficult for her to meet the well-traveled, well-read, well-mannered Americans with whom she could have exchanged *mots d'esprit*, obscure quotations, rare kitchen recipes, reminiscences, and anecdotes. She thought such Americans did not exist. She had a group of European lady friends who, when they gathered around the tea-table, talked of nothing but the barbaric habits of the natives. What disturbed her about Americans was their lack of interest in the things that filled her life—books, poetry, history, and well-turned phrases—their indifference to the virtues she cultivated: moderation, discipline, skepticism, prudence, thrift, patience, and understanding. She was frightened by their noisy and indiscriminate enthusiasms. She lived in the United States eight months a year (she went back to Italy every summer) as resignedly and courageously as the wife of a missionary in an incomprehensible and practically uninhabitable country.[6]

The last touch in that paragraph is the summary gesture in this character sketch: Barzini, Sr., and his wife were colonists in the strictest sense of the word, people who had little to do with the natives, whether these were Italian immigrants or indigenous Americans. It is unsurprising that Barzini, Sr., returned to Italy as a faithful servant of the Mussolini regime, a role he would continue to occupy even after the Duce had been deposed in Rome and the German army had re-installed him as Capo della Repubblica di Salò which from 1943 until the arrival of the American army in 1945 controlled most of Northern Italy.

Luigi Barzini, Jr., lived much of his life between the United States and Italy—for a long time, he revisited America almost every year—interpreting America for Italians and Italy for Americans.

---

[6] Luigi Barzini, Jr., *Americans Are Alone in the World* (1953; New York: The Library Press, 1972) 58.

His best-seller *The Italians* (1964) was an introductory guidebook for Americans who wanted a key to the ideological histories embedded in Italian art and culture. Some years earlier he had written a work intended both for Americans and for everyone else. "The Americans inherited Christendom in 1945 because they not only are able to design and build wonderful machines but can also reproduce them in great quantity, at great speed, and at a low cost" (88). This unexceptionable observation leads him to a memorable vision:

> It took the Americans three years [after the war]—too late to save China and Eastern Europe—before they began to suspect what had happened, that *they were alone in the world* [italics mine], that history was to be shaped by their decisions, the decisions of the President, of the Secretary of State, the generals in the Pentagon, the senators and the representatives. (91)

This categorical vision can be read at two levels: for his readers, it is a standard sample of early Cold War rhetoric; for Barzini himself, it expresses his immersion in transnational space, where Americans may be alone in the world, but they are alone together with the other orphans of history:

> Americans forget that the United States is also an ancient European nation. Morally, if not geographically, she should be placed in the North Sea, with borders touching Great Britain, Normandy, Belgium, Holland, Germany, and the Scandinavian countries, with a long tail reaching into the Mediterranean, where the California vineyards and the sun-baked plains of the Southwest could find room. [...] Now that many Americans have reached a dead end, and the old simple rules have shown themselves to be useful but insufficient, they are looking for some new assurances, for new guides, and they will remember that they are part of a vaster world and that they have never really broken away from an experience which goes back many centuries. (178-179)

A baroque argument for Barzini's personal resolution of the Italian + American question, this transnational brotherhood of orphans appears at the intellectual convergence of parallel lines that recurs frequently in the more hopeful and sentimental of writers on either side of the empty transatlantic space.

AMERICA IS AN ORPHAN

Ignazio Silone foregrounds the emptiness that Italians in Italy share with Italians in the United States. He focuses on survival, which he places within the constricting frame of daily life among the desperately poor. In his first novel *Fontamara* (1929), the narrator pauses during a walk through a half-empty town in the mountains of Abruzzo:

> We stopped to rest for a bit in the shade of the cemetery wall. Against that wall there stood a few mausoleums belonging to peasants who had grown rich in America. Not rich enough to buy a house and land and to live better, but enough for a tomb that after death would make them equal with the gentry.[7]

In the killing fields of transnational space, not only the immigrants but also their dreams and ambitions lie under the monuments of their failure.

Of the Italians to come to America and then return defeated to Italy, none had a sharper disillusion than the poet Emanuel Carnevali. Here he is, sailing up the Hudson:

> This was New York. This was the city we had dreamed so much about, and these were the fabulous skyscrapers. It was one of the great disillusions of my entire unhappy life. These famous skyscrapers were nothing more than great boxes standing upright or on one side, terrifically futile, frightfully irrelevant, so commonplace that one felt he had seen the same thing somewhere else.

---

[7] Ignazio Silone, *Fontamara* (1933; rpt. Milan: Arnoldo Mondadori, 1971) 56.

> This was the long-dreamed of New York, this awful network of fire escapes. This was not the New York we had dreamed of, so dear to the imagination, so cherished among all the hopes a man may hope: this dream of the dreamless, this shelter of the homeless, this impossible city. This miserable panorama before us was one of the greatest cities in the world.[8]

"This miserable panorama before us was one of the greatest cities in the world." That remarkable sentence is a sarcastic oxymoron opened up, unfolded, and splayed before us like the innards of a fish. It is a mistake to read such prose as simply a fortunate example of immigrant writing. This prose strikes at the heart of human condition and belongs to world literature. Carnevali recognizes the massive disillusion (*delusione* in Italian) of this moment on the Hudson River as a moment of naked revelation. Behold the transnational space. Its towering illusions collapse under the gaze of the clear-eyed pilgrim.

Possibly the best known of Carnevali's poems makes it clear that he had found his world orphanage in America. After his meteoric career as a young poet in his early twenties, Carnevali returned to Italy desperately ill, filled with a sarcastic hope:

> Italy is a little family;
> America is an orphan,
> Independent and arrogant,
> Crazy and sublime,
> Riding headlong in a mad run which she calls progress.
> Tremendously laborious America,
> Builder of the Mechanical cities
> But in the hurry people forget to love;
> But in the hurry one drops and loses kindness.

---

[8] Emanuel Carnevali, *The Autobiography of Emanuel Carnevali*, compiled and prefaced by Kay Boyle (New York: Horizon, 1967) 73.

> And hunger is the patrimony of the emigrant;
> Hunger, desolate and squalid —
> For the fatherland,
> For bread and for women, both dear.
> America, you gather the hungry people
> And give them new hungers for old ones (198).

These new hungers are what he brought back with him to Italy:

> I have come back and found you
> All new and friendly, O Fatherland!
> I have come back with a great burden,
> With the experience of America in my head —
> My head which now no longer beats the stars.
>
> O Italy, O great shoe, do not
> Kick me away again! (201).

While feelings run both east and west across the transnational void, their most striking characteristics are their mutual similarities. Almost as striking as "America is an orphan" is the line that precedes it: "Italy is a little family," which speaks from the perspective of the veteran who has seen New York and Chicago, "Tremendously laborious America/ Builder of Mechanical cities." This little family is not the Italy that the Risorgimento aimed to build, but rather the Italy that the returning migrant sees with his American eyes.

The Italian American in Italy

In the 1920s and 1930s, the sense of a universal homelessness begins to spread. In 1936, the Sicilian American writer Jerre Mangione, still a young man, decides to visit the Sicily that his parents had left behind. Before Mangione embarks, his friend Carlo Tresca, the most notorious Italian anarchist in America, throws him a going-away party, to which many well-known radicals are invited. By this time, Tresca is already a target of Mussolini's, and Mangione can't help wondering whether there are any Fascist informers hiding among the guests at this party. But he buries his doubts and concentrates upon family investigations. His uncle Stefano in Rochester, New York, has charged him particularly to ask after Zio Vincenzo, a relative who returned to Sicily some years earlier, giving shape to an ambition that Stefano has been harboring for himself. Mangione visits Agrigento and finds Zio Vincenzo. They pack a lunch and take a bus out to the Valley of the Temples. "There," he writes, "with our backs resting against a column of the Temple of Concordia and our eyes on the sea, we ate and conversed."

> [Vincenzo] asked about his old friends [in Rochester] and wanted to know if Uncle Stefano was still talking of returning to Sicily. I told him it was still his dream; in Rochester he would never stop feeling like a foreigner.
> "I used to feel that way there," [Zio Vincenzo] said. "But actually I feel much more foreign here. Tell Stefano to stay where he is. Things have changed here. There is still beauty, of course, especially in the spring when this valley is filled with wildflowers, but I find that beauty is not enough for me. The neighborhood in Rochester where I lived is far from beautiful, but I would rather be there. There is a blight on all of Italy and it seems to be getting worse. The newspapers claim there won't be another war, but I don't believe it. I can see it coming closer all the time, the biggest war the world has ever known, and I curse the day when I decided to come back to this benighted land."[9]

Here the narrator enters a transoceanic hall of mirrors. He has come to Italy with a vast curiosity that in short order receives an abrupt reply. He sees that his uncle misses "his old cronies" and, more important, "the American prerogative of speaking one's mind without fear of being reported to the authorities as a subversive."

---

[9] Jerre Mangione, *An Ethnic at Large: A Memoir of America in the Thirties and Forties* (New York: G.P. Putnam's Sons, 1978), 186-187.

Now that he is actually in Italy, he finds himself continually surrounded by informers, some of them his own relatives, who are shocked to learn that he has written critically of the regime and of its great writers, including Luigi Pirandello. He discovers that his letters are being opened and read before he has received them. "Perhaps they think you are American spy," his cousin suggests. This terrifies him. "I bitterly pictured myself answering [my] letters from a Fascist jail cell." His cousin tries to reassure him. "If they wanted to nab you, they would have by now. They must have decided you aren't a spy" (188-189). His distress does not abate, however, and it leads to something he finds even more unsettling:

> The opened letters were not my only concern. I was also upset by the frequency with which Italians mistook me for a native. In the fever of my anxiety, I began to feel I was gradually losing my identity as an American. The most shattering of these experiences took place in the Palermo train station when an elderly, well-dressed traveler, to whom I had turned for assistance in unraveling the mysteries of the timetable for Rome, began berating me for trying to make a fool of him by pretending I was a foreigner. (189)

Though Mangione tries desperately to explain himself, even showing the man his American passport, the man just grows angrier. "He left without apologizing, still angry, declaring at the top of his voice that Americans had no business being in Italy" (189). After that, he speaks in broken Italian and wears loud neckties, hoping to make it clear he is not an Italian. "Although I hungrily sought the company of American tourists as a means of asserting my birthright, at times they only emphasized my sensation of not really being one of them" (190). Though he continues his travels, visiting Florence and Venice, he never quite recovers from this loss of "birthright" and leaves for America sooner than he had planned. This episode is a bitter foreshadowing of what was about to happen when the war began. Italian Americans, many like Zio Vincenzo, had kept warm in their hearts an image of Italy, now furbished with the glory of Mussolini's relentless publicity about Fascism's achievements. When Mussolini declared war on the United States three days after the bombing of Pearl Harbor, he expected Italians to return to Italy and fight for their "fatherland," but things had changed. Almost immediately, Uncle Sam told Italian Americans to stop speaking the "enemy's language" and to "speak American" instead. Many of them were rounded up and sent to internment camps. Italy, that had stood behind Italian Americans in New Orleans in 1891, now wanted them to fight against the country where their children had been born. They did not heed the appeal. In the end, Mussolini felt betrayed, and the Italian Americans felt abandoned.

RE-HOMING

In the postwar transnational space, the paranoia and despair of wartime seemed to have become chronic conditions. In the United States, the McCarthy purges caused many Americans, Italian Americans among them, to repent and to eradicate their prewar political affiliations. Vito Marcantonio, the Socialist who represented Italian Harlem in the House of Representatives, saw his career go down in a storm of redbaiting when he ran for Mayor of New York City in 1950. Unions began to weaken and wither in the deadening regressive atmosphere of the 1950s. In Italy, the Italian Americans came to be framed by their participation in the American Army that had invaded Italy in the 1940s. These historical transformations registered in the imaginations of Italian Americans and Italians as betrayals, in a map of reflections, projects, and actual treasons too complex to map and best registered in the fantasy world of fable.

The best portrait of this ideological hall of mirrors is Leonardo Sciascia's *Candido, ovvero un sogno fatto in Sicilia*.[10] The eponymous hero of this novel is born in the heart of the particular transnational situation we have been following:

---

[10] *Candido, ovvero un sogno fatto in Sicilia* (Turin: Einaudi, 1977); *Candido, or A Dream Dreamed in Sicily*, trans. Adrienne Foulke (New York: Harcourt Brace Jovanovich, 1979).

Candido Munafò was born on the night of July 9-10, 1943, in a grotto that opened, wide and deep, at the foot of a hillside of olive trees. Nothing was easier that to be born in a grotto or in a stable that summer and especially that night in Sicily, as it was fought over by the American Seventh Army under General Patton, the British Eighth Army under General Montgomery, the Hermann Goering Division, and several almost invisible Italian regiments (3).

"Born in a grotto" in the middle of an epic transnational battle—American, British, German, Italian—led by famous commanders—Patton, Montgomery, Goering, and the invisible Italian—Candido's biblical and epic qualifications are ironic: "There was ... no supernatural or premonitory sign in Candido Munafò's being born in a grotto" nor in any of other accidents of his birth. This is a fable that begins, at least, in real time, on a specific historical date, and proceeds to weave its peculiar notions on ideological themes richly familiar to readers who had lived through this period.

The decisive encounter occurs between the lawyer Munafò (Candido's father) and John H. Dykes (the American captain). The lawyer's family is bereft of everything, especially proper food for the baby.

> The Captain was moved; he had powdered milk, condensed milk, evaporated milk, sugar, coffee, oatmeal, graham crackers, and canned meat sent to the house. Manna from Heaven, even for a house with a larder as well-supplied as was that of Munafò (10).

This munificence draws a visit from the lawyer, who discovers that Captain Dykes in civilian life is a professor of Italian literature in a university. A long-lost twin indeed. And there's more: "He spoke of his mother.... His mother was a Sicilian; from a village nearby, only fifteen kilometers away." Though the lawyer has no luck finding any relatives for the captain, he tells his wife of his discovery, uttering the fateful cliché "It's a small world." Signora Munafò promptly concurs.

> She wished ultimately to make the world even smaller by inviting Captain John H. Dykes to dinner. The *H* stood for Hamlet, a revelation that so enchanted Maria Grazia that when they had reached a point of sufficient familiarity, she ended up calling the Captain simply "Hamlet." This pleased the Captain greatly, for, he said, this was what his mother used to call him (10).

These are all steps in a magical transformation suggestive of Gabriel Garcia Marquez. Next step:

> thanks to the milk and other prodigious American foodstuffs, Candido was becoming quite different from the swarthy baby he had been in the first days of his life; he was growing both rosy and blond. More and more, he resembled John H. Dykes.

This resemblance, plus the growing friendship between Maria Grazia and Captain Dykes leads the lawyer to a strange suspicion: that John H. Dykes might be the father of Candido," a physical impossibility.[11] Nonetheless, it leads to a divorce. Maria Grazia marries Dykes and moves to the United States. The divorce is the most Voltairean moment in this novel named for Voltaire's *Candide*. Neither parent wants the child but both vehemently assert their desire to raise him. The lawyer "wins."

> With due respect for law and appearance, the lawyer Munafò appeared to be vindictively pleased, vindictively happy to have won the match to keep Candido himself, while Maria Grazia appeared dolorous in defeat. However, the person truly defeated was the lawyer: he was forced to keep the son he did not love, the son he

---

[11] The provenance of Captain Dykes's mother in a village fifteen miles away might, of course, contain enough genetic material to account for Candido's striking resemblance to Dykes, but no one scouts this possibility. The lawyer particularly obsesses over a more direct genetic line, even though there is no chance of events that would have caused it.

could not feel was his son, and whom, unspeakably, in his secret rage, he did not call "Candido" but "the American" (18).

Candido, in accordance with his name, is remarkably forthright. Overhearing one of his father's clients confess to the lawyer that he has in fact committed a murder for which a lieutenant of Carabinieri had arrested another person, Candido hastens to tell the lieutenant's son, his nursery school classmate, that his father the lawyer has made a mistake and that the lieutenant is innocent. "Pandemonium ensued" (24). In short order, the lawyer Munafò commits suicide, leaving Candido for all practical purposes an orphan. His mother does not want him. So Candido's father's maid and his Fascist-turned-Demochristian politician grandfather take him on. This is the first in a series of re-homings (a practice developed to deal with failed pet adoptions; the name is now used in dealing with unwanted children as well).

Like many a chastened pit bull and Pomeranian, Candido learns to thrive by respecting his new owners and his own nature. The orphaned Sicilian who becomes an American without leaving Sicily is a fantasy that had its own brief half-life in postwar Sicily, where some inhabitants wished for their island to become the 49th State.

That solution soon enough became a curiosity. Instead of becoming Americans by joining the United States, the Italians became Europeans, first by enthusiastically accepting American aid in all its forms, from powdered milk to Otis elevators, later by joining the European Union, a plausible double to the American confederation. The songwriter Gianni Buoncompagni acidly summarizes the situation:

> E se vai a cercar fortuna in America
> Ti accorgi che l'America sta qua.[12]

---

[12] Gianni Buoncompagni (lyrics), Toto Cutugno (music)."Una Domenica Italiana," a song that satirizes the Italians' addiction to American food, television, and other habits of daily life. See Barbara Alfano, *The Mirage of America in Contemporary Italian Literature* (Toronto: University of Toronto Press, 2013). Alfano's

> [And if you go to seek your fortune in America,
> you realize that America's right here.]

This is another story. The orphanage twins are accustomed to one another by now, their bitterness amounting to sarcasms and other forms of wit and flirtation they use when, visiting Torino, they drink at the gleaming Bar Gramsci.

---

contemporary Italian literature begins just about where the bulk of this essay concludes.

Postscript 2018

After Transnational Space

When I wrote this essay on transnational space in 2015, the concept of setting space free of laws and boundaries seemed to promise new forms of liberation and new spaces for exploration, even (and especially) within spaces we had long been accustomed to negotiate under restrictions and laws that belonged to a massive regime of inherited arrangements.

This promise began to fall under shadows in real time, even as I was tracing its rhythms of recurrence in the works I was studying. Looking back on the prophecies of the years that struggles of youth and of the unremitting conflicts that surrounded us had been an exercise that gave us plenty of occasions for hope. But the terrors of our endless wars have provided us with at least as many occasions for caution and doubt.

We are now faced with the prospect of an administration in Washington that, whether it succeeds or fails, will certainly have left us with enough fresh motives of doubt that will, inevitably, color our visions of the future.

Italian writers have for a long time specialized in providing us with scenarios for such visions. After considering the changes that have been taking place, I have chosen a recent example, written by an unusually well-informed narrator, Andrea Camilleri. *The Sacco Gang* (2013) paints an unremitting portrait of how the *malavita*, well-entrenched in Sicilian life, deploys its formidable resources to pursue and obstruct the actions of law-abiding businessmen, sometimes for decades.

The title is ironic. The Saccos are not a gang. They are a family business, built patiently across three generations, by a clan of law-abiding businessmen who, even under the violent duress imposed upon them by the Mafia, do not fail to fight back within the boundaries of the law. The irony goes further, of course.

To the Mafia, the Saccos *are* a gang. Their refusal to play by Mafia rules hobbles them. The Mafia, by contrast, is hobbled only by its unwillingness to join the economy of international rules and institutions.

Camilleri tells the story of the struggle between the Saccos and the Mafia with no pretense of even-handedness. His sympathy is all on the side of the Sacco family, whom he ironically calls a gang.

They are not a gang, except in the eyes of their oppressors. Camilleri is at great pains to show them as a law-abiding agricultural concern whose principals are all members of a single clan. The clan has risen in local prominence gradually across three generations, and, as the narrative opens, they are a successful agricultural concern, still a strong and well-integrated family presence in local commercial life. Three of Luigi's sons have spent long sojourns in America, earning and saving money, and they have returned to Raffadali to fight in the First World War. After the conflict ends, they are united in their town. One of Luigi's sons, Girolamo, was injured in the war, but the other four are all good earners

In an "Author's Note" at the end of this volume, Andrea Camilleri writes:

> I've been able to tell this utterly true story only because Giovanni Sacco, one of Girolamo's children, asked me to recount the vicissitudes his family lived through, and provided me with official documents, family writings and correspondences, and minutes of the trials.
>
> I would therefore like to thank him with all my heart and dedicate this book to his memory.
>
> I've limited myself only to changing a name or two here and there and using false initials.
>
> I have tried to show, through this "Western of things of ours"—to use one of Sciascia's titles—how the Mafia not only kills, but in those cases where the state does missing, is also able to shape and irreparably upend people's lives.
>
> A.C.

This blunt postscript summarizes the state of the evidence under consideration, at the same time that it asserts Camilleri's attitude, indeed his humility, before it. Camilleri thus succeeds in dramatizing the scene of composition with an awesome chill.

What we see, across this long horizon, is the growing power of large interests and the complementary shrinkage of smaller powers, whether these belong to localities, minorities, or individuals. *Mere* individuals, we might say, did it not seem a vain piety in the face of the transformations in social and economic structures that proceed apace, not only in the Italian provinces these days, but across the face of Europe and of what we used to called the "civilized world" —an expression that seems more and more an awkward survival from another time.

This is not the first moment that a new and larger civility has seemed to disappear under the brutal fists of conspiracy and greed. One can hope this will be a brief and awkward interruption in a long and wider peace, a prelude to a larger calm, an even global interlude.

Index

1980 Census 3, 16, 17
Agnelli Foundation 13
American Commissioner of Labor 14
Anarchism, 35, 37-43
Ancestry.com, 65, 88-90, 94-95, 98, 99
Associazione Nazionale Comuni Italiani (ANCI), 73

Bargo dei Borghi Competition, 66, 73, 74, 77
Barolini, Helen 6, 25
Bassetti, Piero 22
Barzini Jr., Luigi 112-115
    Americans Are Alone in the World, 113, *The Italians* 114
Barzini Sr., Luigi 112
Bava-Beccaris, Fiorenzo 111
Berlusconi, Silvio 103
Bresci, Gaetano 111
Buoncompagni, Gianni 123-124

Cacioppo, Giuseppe, 96
Campanilismo, 60
Candeloro, Dominic 6
Capra, Francesco (Frank) 27
Carnevali, Emanuel 115-117, *The Autobiography of Emanuel Carnevali* 116
Chiesa della Carmine, 69, 73
Chiesa San Giorgio, 69
Circofi, 95-96
Citizen researchers, 58, 83, 97, 100-101
Columbus Day Parade 103
Corriere d'America 112
Covello, Leonardo 4, 5, 8, 9, 10

D'Agostino, Guido 9
D'Angelo, Pascal 112-115
De Amicis, Edmondo 110-111
DeVellis, Claudio 1
Digital scholarship, 57-58, 99-102
Do the Right Thing 20
Eco, Umbero, 49-50
educato 4, 11
Elizabeth Street, New York, 60-61, 65, 69
Facebook, 76-79
Fascism 35, 46-50, 106
Ferragamo, Salvatore 37-38, 41, 43-45
Festa deill'Unità, 73
figura 21, 26
Fischer, Michael M.J. 27, 28
Fogli di famiglia, 63
Folklore, 99
Freud, Sigmund 26

G.I. Bill 12
Gabaccia, Donna 106-107
Gagliano, Nicholas, 87, n. 105, 97, 99, 101
Galleani, Luigi 37-39, 45
Gambino, Richard 3, 4, 13, 15
Genealogists, 81-98, 100-101
Google Books, 62

Interrogations into Italian-American Studies
The Francesco and Mary Giambelli Foundation Lectures Series (2020)

INDEX

Google Scholar, 62
Google Search, 53, 65; Google Image Search 67-70
Great Migration 105-106
Greater Rockford Italian American Association, 84
Greeley, Andrew 3, 13, 16

iIlliteracy rate 5
"In Dreams Begin Responsibilities" 2
istruito 4, 12
ITA-SAMBUCA-DI-SICILIA, 91-97
Italianita 23
Italicita 22, 23

Johnson-Reed Act 45
Jones, Jacqueline, 81-82
La Voce di Sambuca, 54, 85-86, 96
Lee, Spike 20
Lista della leva, 63
Little Italy, 3

Maastricht Treaty 104
Mangione, Jerre 117-120
Marcantonio, Vito 120
Moustache Pete 6-8; 28-33
Museo Pitrè, 61
Mussolini, Benito 117, 119
MySpace, 66

National Opinion Research Institute 13
Nativism 35, 43-46
Navarro della Miraglia, 56, n. 29, 66, 72

Navarro, Vincent, 66
New Orleans lynching 107

Oral history, 64

Palermo, Sicily, 61
Parrinello, Will, 3
Pirandello, Luigi 119
Pitre, Giuseppe, 61, 77
Pro Loco Fenicia, 74, 76
Putnam, Lara, 58

"Responsibilities" 1, 2
Risorgimento 104-105
Rockford, Illinois, 84, 85, 90, 96
Rogers, Will 48
Rootsweb, 91-95

Sacco, Nicola 37-43, 45, 47
Sambuca Club, 84, 86, 96, 95-96, 97, 98
Schneider, Jane and Peter, 54-56, 61
Schwartz, Delmore 1, 24
Sciacca, Sicily, 61
Sciascia, Leonardo 69, 120-123, *Candido, or A Dream Dreamed in Sicily* 121-123Smith, Alison, 84
Silone, Ignazio 115, *Fontamara* 115-116
social classes 4
Somogyi, Stefano, 61
SS Maria della Udienza, 72

Teatro L'Idea, 68, 74
Tenney, Justine 1

The Chicago Oral History
    Project 6
The Dream Book 6
The Great Depression 12, 18
The Heart is the Teacher 9
The Partisan Review 2
*The Social Background of the
    Ital-American School Child*
    4
*The Southern Question
    (Questione Meridionale*
Tourism, 71, 73, 74, 75, 94, 99
Transitional space 107-109
Tresca, Carlo 117-118
Trump, Donald 35, 40, 45-48

U.S. Immigration Report
    1910 14
Umbertina 25

Valdinocci, Carlo 40
Vanzetti, Bartolomeo 37-43,
    45
Vecoli, Rudolph 15, 16
Vicoli saraceni (sette veneddi),
    69
Vigo Lodge, Order of Sons of
    Italy, 96
Villamaura 56, 61, n. 21
Viscusi, Robert 1

Webpages, 80-81
Wikipedia, 66
World War II 12, 18, 116

Yeats, William Butler 1, 2, 28
YouTube, 70-75

SAGGISTICA

Taking its name from the Italian—which means essays, essay writing, or non-fiction—*Saggisitca* is a referred book series dedicated to the study of all topics and cultural productions that fall under what we might consider that larger umbrella of all things Italian and Italian/American.

Vito Zagarrio
The "Un-Happy Ending": Re-viewing The Cinema of Frank Capra. 2011. ISBN 978-1-59954-005-4. Volume 1.

Paolo A. Giordano, Editor
The Hyphenate Writer and The Legacy of Exile. 2010. ISBN 978-1-59954-007-8. Volume 2.

Dennis Barone
America / Trattabili. 2011. ISBN 978-1-59954-018-4. Volume 3.

Fred L. Gardaphè
The Art of Reading Italian Americana. 2011. ISBN 978-1-59954-019-1. Volume 4.

Anthony Julian Tamburri
Re-viewing Italian Americana: Generalities and Specificities on Cinema. 2011. ISBN 978-1-59954-020-7. Volume 5.

Sheryl Lynn Postman
An Italian Writer's Journey through American Realities: Giose Rimanelli's English Novels. "The most tormented decade of America: the 60s" ISBN 978-1-59954-034-4. Volume 6.

Luigi Fontanella
Migrating Words: Italian Writers in the United States. 2012. ISBN 978-1-59954-041-2. Volume 7.

Peter Covino & Dennis Barone, Editors
Essays on Italian American Literature and Culture. 2012. ISBN 978-1-59954-035-1. Volume 8.

Gianfranco Viesti
Italy at the Crossroads. 2012. ISBN 978-1-59954-071-9. Volume 9.

Peter Carravetta, Editor
Discourse Boundary Creation (LOGOS TOPOS POIESIS): A Festschrift in Honor of Paolo Valesio. ISBN 978-1-59954-036-8. Volume 10.

Antonio Vitti and Anthony Julian Tamburri, Editors
Europe, Italy, and the Mediterranean. ISBN 978-1-59954-073-3. Volume 11.

Vincenzo Scotti
Pax Mafiosa or War: Twenty Years after the Palermo Massacres. 2012. ISBN 978-1-59954-074-0. Volume 12.

Anthony Julian Tamburri, Editor
Meditations on Identity. Meditazioni su identità. ISBN 978-1-59954-082-5. Volume 13.

Peter Carravetta, Editor
Theater of the Mind, Stage of History. A Festschrift in Honor of Mario Mignone. ISBN 978-1-59954-083-2. Volume 14.

Lorenzo Del Boca
Italy's Lies. Debunking History's Lies So That Italy Might Become A "Normal Country". ISBN 978-1-59954-084-9. Volume 15.

George Guida
Spectacles of Themselves. Essays in Italian American Popular Culture and Literature. ISBN 978-1-59954-090-0. Volume 16.

Antonio Vitti and Anthony Julian Tamburri, Editors
Mare Nostrum: prospettive di un dialogo tra alterità e mediterraneità. ISBN 978-1-59954-100-6. Volume 17.

Patrizia Salvetti
Rope and Soap. Lynchings of Italians in the United States. ISBN 978-1-59954-101-3. Volume 18.

Sheryl Lynn Postman and Anthony Julian Tamburri, Editors
Re-reading Rimanelli in America: Six Decades in the United States. ISBN 978-1-59954-102-0. Volume 19.

Pasquale Verdicchio
Bound by Distance. Rethinking Nationalism Through the Italian Diaspora. ISBN 978-1-59954-103-7. Volume 20.

Peter Carravetta
After Identity. Migration, Critique, Italian American Culture. ISBN 978-1-59954-072-6. Volume 21.

Antonio Vitti and Anthony Julian Tamburri, Editors
The Mediterranean As Seen by Insiders and Outsiders. ISBN 978-1-59954-107-5. Volume 22.

Eugenio Ragni
Giose 1959. Un "Suicidio" Annunciato. American Culture. ISBN 978-1-59954-109-9. Volume 23.

Quinto Antonelli
Intimate History of the Great War: Letters, Diaries, and Memoirs from Soldiers on the Front. ISBN 978-1-59954-111-2. Volume 24.

Antonio Vitti and Anthony Julian Tamburri, Editors
The Mediterranean Dreamed and Lived by Insiders and Outsiders. ISBN 978-1-59954-115-0. Volume 25.

Sabrina Vellucci and Carla Francellini, Editors
   Re-Mapping Italian America: Places, Cultures, Identities. ISBN 978-1-59954-116-7. Volume 26.
Stephen J. Belluscio
   Garibaldi M. Lapolla: A Study of His Novels. ISBN 978-1-59954-125-9. Volume 27.
Antonio Vitti and Anthony Julian Tamburri, Editors
   The Representation of the Mediterranean World by Insiders and Outsiders. ISBN 978-1-59954-113-6. Volume 28.
Philip Balma and Giovanni Spani, eds. *Translating For (And From) The Italian Screen: Dubbing And Subtitles.* ISBN 978-1-59954-141-9. Volume 29.
Antonio Vitti and Anthony Julian Tamburri, Editors
   The Representation of the Mediterranean World by Insiders and Outsiders. ISBN 978-1-59954-142-6. Volume 30.
Anthony Julian Tamburri, Editor. *Interrogations into Italian-American Studies.* The Francesco and Mary Giambelli Foundation Lectures. ISBN 978-1-59954-143-3. Volume 31.

www.ingramcontent.com/pod-product-compliance
Lightning Source LLC
Chambersburg PA
CBHW062110080426
42734CB00012B/2813